ALONG THE WAY

BY
DONALD N. BASTIAN

Light and Life Press
Winona Lake, Indiana 46590

Printed in the United States of America
by Light and Life Press, Winona Lake, Indiana 46590

ISBN: 0-89367-008-1

Dedication

To three esteemed congregations:
a small Free Methodist Church
in Lexington, Kentucky;
a medium-sized one
in New Westminster, B. C., Canada;
and a large one in Greenville, Illinois.

Contents

Introduction

For twenty-one years I was a pastor, first in Lexington, Kentucky, then in New Westminster, B.C., Canada, and finally in Greenville, Illinois. During those years, few days passed when I was not closeted with some other mortal, sharing deeply in the issues of life.

You might be surprised at the range of concerns people bring to pastors.

I remember a fourteen-year-old lad who came to share a secret. He was in love. He read from a copy of the Song of Solomon, "Many waters cannot quench love, neither can the floods drown it." The words described his feelings.

I wasn't startled by what he told me. The disclosure filled me with a sense of awe. Here was a young man experiencing for the first time feelings strong enough to be able later to fuel a life-long commitment to a woman. His judgment would mature with the years, but his feelings would never be a great deal stronger.

His parents were well able to coach him through this crucial period of his life. Mine was the privilege of receiving his confidence and responding appropriately. In my heart I thanked God for the wonder of what he told me.

It wasn't so easy to respond to the twenty-three-year-old man just released from the penitentiary. He came late one night. He blew smoke in my face and assulted my ears with expressions not commonly heard in civil conversation. He was testing me to see if I cared as much as someone in my profession was supposed to, and I knew it. Nothing came of our talk.

Between these two extremes there was a great

variety. Aged people articulated their loneliness. (Young people often did too.) The bereaved often shared their memories. Young married couples hit snags they had not foreseen and asked for help. Sometimes people wanted to share their joy. There were burdens of shame to unload in the presence of some trusted mortal. None of this was done easily.

I'm convinced that almost all people who seek out pastors are pilgrims. That doesn't mean they are super pious or otherworldly. But they sense, however vaguely, that life is a journey to a destination, and it is the destination that gives the present moment significance. Whether they are brought by their aspirings or their failures, this is what they have in common.

Whenever I listened well, I listened also as a pilgrim. I wasn't just a carefully programmed listening machine. I, too, was on a journey. My history was also marked by aspirations and perplexities and failures. Therefore, I could see something of myself in everyone to whom I listened. We were meeting along the way.

What this book contains is a bit of the cerebral side of a few of those conversations. Chapters are not built often on specific situations. But, often after a serious conversation, I was moved to write by the questions people asked, the uncertainies they shared, or the answers the Bible offered.

Perhaps as you read, you will find yourself mirrored here or there. Or you may discover in what I have intended to be a simple development of some biblical idea an answer to a question you have. I hope so. And, if you do, you and I will also meet along the way.

— Donald M. Bastian

Chapter 1

The Real Robert Sandin

Robert Sandin, twenty-two, has fine blond locks that fall just below his ear lobes, and when he turns his head suddenly they don't quite keep pace.

His dress is predictable: faded jeans and a dark turtleneck seven days a week.

Sandin's friends like him. He adapts fairly easily to new situations, and he's quick with a quip.

What his friends don't know is that when he's alone he fights depression. Sometimes this dark cloud hangs over him for hours, sometimes a few days.

His life-style, though, is freewheeling. He eats when he feels like it (often) and sleeps when he wants to (late in the morning, never before midnight). People bound by clocks and logic are not living, he thinks.

Robert Sandin — the private one — not only fights depression; he cries, too. He did so the first time he came to see me. He stiffened his chin to control the quaver in his voice.

Reading from notes on the back of an envelope,

glancing down at them and then staring across at the wall, he recited a list of problems.

When he finished this painful recital, turning his palms upward in a sudden gesture of distress, he said, "I don't know what's bothering me."

Robert Sandin is a professing Christian. He's not sure what he believes about people and human relationships, but he says he believes in Christ. He may be mistaken, but he's not bluffing. He believes he believes.

Robert's mind is like a file drawer, teeming with a ten-year collection of papers — minus dividers and without order. There are sheets from popular songs, ditties from TV commercials, one-liner ideas from Sartre and Russell, whom he's never read, and a few tidy pages from the Bible.

He's accumulated them, but he doesn't know how to sort them. He doesn't know which to throw away, which to keep. If he opens the drawer suddenly, he doesn't know which will tumble out first this time. He talks about it, and his lower lids brim with tears.

How did Robert Sandin get this way?

His parents believed a child should make as many of his own decisions as early as possible. They said this was good psychology. They were quite busy.

Robert used to come in from school when he was a child, drop down in front of the TV, tune out Reality Center and tune in Fantasy City. This way he collected a head full of guns, intrigue, twisted comedy, fast talk, sex, and cute ditties about bathroom tissues.

Later, when he got his own record player, he added to the assortment disconnected lines from the Beatles, plaintive strains from Bob Dylan, and snatches of this and that from a host of teenage idols.

When Robert Sandin talks about earlier days in his life, he talks mostly about his peers. When he joked, they were his audience; when he attempted serious talk, it was in dialogue with them.

But he says he's a Christian. He believes he believes. Should he be told, "Don't worry, you're just growing up"? (He's twenty-two, remember.) Should he be scorned? (He's in anguish now.) What should he be told to do?

I can tell you what Robert Sandin is doing. He's trying to interact honestly with a couple of adults who find life meaningful. It's hard work. He's trying to tune in again on the church, too. At least there they read the Scriptures and pray to God.

But besides, he's reading the Gospel of John nightly — on his knees. When he gets through once, he's going to start through again. He's promised.

There's good reason for him to read John. It's written to elicit faith not only in the heart but in the head as well (20:30, 31). Robert needs more than just to feel better. He needs some unifying commitment — a faith by which he can sort out the clutter of his filing-drawer mind.

The Gospel of John will do it if given a chance. In it, Jesus Christ is the key to reality. For reality, John uses the word *truth,* and Robert needs urgently to be put in touch with truth.

There are hard days ahead for Robert Sandin. But already he's not blaming his parents and the church for the mess he's in. He's even beginning to recognize falseness in his own life, and he's making some decisions to get himself off dead center.

Light is beginning to turn on in Sandin's dark and cluttered mind — *the* Light, in fact.

Chapter 2

If Jesus Could Sigh — Why Can't We?

"The Jesus I hear about in church," said a young woman, "is too plastic. He seems almost phony."

The way Jesus is talked about in church may sometimes make Him seem unreal. But the way He's talked about in the Gospels doesn't. There His humanity is lifelike.

Take Mark 8:11-13. The Pharisees were trying to get Jesus to do something spectacular. "Show us a sign from heaven." It would make believers of them, they implied; but they didn't mean it.

Jesus sighed deeply in spirit and said, "Why does this generation seek a sign?"

We can understand His feelings. We know what it's like to sigh.

A sigh is a profoundly human response to all sorts of hurts — especially the kind that won't let up and can't easily be put into words.

A widower, nursing a private grief which he thinks everyone else has forgotten, sucks in a quick, deep breath and lets it out slowly. He scarcely realizes what he has done.

Speaking about the darker side of the believer's earthly life, Paul said, "We ourselves, who have the first fruits of the Spirit, groan inwardly as we wait for adoption as sons" (Romans 8:23, RSV). *(Groan* here and *sigh* in Mark are derived from the same Greek word.)

Jesus' anguish under the badgering of the religious leaders must have been deep and wrenching. It brought forth a sigh-groan.

Why such hurt?

In Him, God had come among men to rule them. That's what Mark means when he talks about the kingdom. Jesus healed and taught and sweated, sometimes to near exhaustion, to establish this rule.

Yet, even His disciples didn't understand. They had seen a long series of miracles, but they were dense. He chided them: "Having eyes, do you not see?"

His enemies were worse than dense. They knew about the miracles too, but they met His works with hostility. They intended *not* to understand.

With friends so dull, and enemies so adverse, what could He do but sigh?

To Mark, Jesus was no superstar — a topflight entertainer whose act wasn't going over. He was a true man living a true life with its share of true hurts.

(He was true God, too, but that side of things must be taken up at another time.)

What shall we do with this episode from Jesus' life? Of what use is it to us?

We must not use it to excuse ourselves for living discontented lives. That kind of living, too, is filled with sighs. But Jesus was not a heavy-spirited person, impatient over little annoyances.

There are traces of humor in His words. His picture of a man trying to remove a speck of sawdust from another's eye while a great plank jutted from his own is not likely from the mind of a heavy-spirited person.

We can do something better with this episode. We can use it to help us admit that life has its inescapable frustrations. It is human to sigh — even for the person who lives close to God. This is a fact we shouldn't ignore.

What if we do ignore it?

Here's a store clerk, ridden by his boss at work and plagued by financial stresses at home. He can't admit what's going on inside him because he thinks it would mar his Christian example. He's now recovering from a bleeding ulcer.

Maybe it won't be anything so dramatic as a bleeding ulcer that signals to us our vulnerability to life. But if we don't permit ourselves to be fully human — which may include sighing — we'll be in no frame of mind to lay hold of God's grace for hurts.

The psalmists have something to teach us here. "O, Lord, all my lament lies open before thee and my sighing is no secret to thee" (Psalm 38:9, *NEB*). Jesus' inner life was nourished by the psalms. He must have known this one.

We can also use the episode to see the profile of our own commitment to God. Like a mirror it reflects us.

Jesus sighed because men were blind when

God's power was evident among them. He hurt because God wanted to establish His rule in them and they were saying no.

It raises the question, What sort of thing makes us sigh? The mistake on the bank statement in today's mail? The spot on a suit that the cleaners didn't get out?

These things, too, are the stuff of life. They're annoyances. But, by Jesus' example, there must be bigger things to sigh over.

The young husband down the street — he knows his wife is different since her conversion, but he seems to remain blind to his own need. The high school class — they're bright and zesty, but we want them to come alive to Jesus.

Needs like this should make us sigh.

We don't need *Superstar* to show us the humanness of Jesus. Mark does it more clearly and without distortion.

We need to expose ourselves to the full range of His humanity. Otherwise, He will seem unreal to us. How then can we avoid representing Him as plastic to others?

Here's how: Nudge up close to Jesus as Mark pictures Him. Listen to the sound of His sighing.

If He could sigh, why can't we? And, if in spite of His hurt, He could keep a straight course in the service of His Father, why can't we?

Chapter 3

Antidote to Anxiety

The trouble with anxiety is that we usually don't know when we have it. Or it has us. The doctor detects it in our symptoms, our friends in our faces, and our families in our mirthless spirits. But we can't see it.

All we know — when we can bring ourselves to think about it — is that a dark cloud on our horizon refuses to go away. We fear it, though we don't know why. Does it forebode health failure, loss of friends, financial embarrassment, family troubles? A long list is possible.

One problem with anxiety is that it has a contagious quality to it. Someone comes home from work tense, worried. Soon the whole family has caught the mood. Home becomes the place of the black cloud.

It is contagious enough so that, living in the world, we are always in peril of catching the world's anxiety. There's a lot of it around and many of us catch it.

Is there any antidote?

Here's Peter's word to Christians in distress. They had already been scattered for their faith, and more trouble was on the horizon. Peter said: "Cast all your anxieties on him, for he cares about you" (I Peter 5:7, RSV).

The most important element in our struggle with this terror of our times is the notion we have of God. If He's only the "Man Upstairs" we're up against it, for He may not really know what goes on downstairs where we live. Or He may not be able to do much, if He knows.

But if He's the God and Father of our Lord Jesus Christ, that's different. He's the God *we* may call "Father" as Jesus did. He's personal, near. And He cares!

So whenever anxiety builds up on us, we should ask ourselves: Am I living as though I have to keep the whole universe going by myself? There's not much faith in that stance. The first need in coping with anxiety is a renewal of genuine faith.

Faith matters, but it has a dimension easily overlooked. The God in whom we trust has made us managers of our own lives, a lofty though perilous assignment. To have faith in the face of anxiety may involve asking ourselves some questions about how we're managing.

Am I anxious because my life values are wrong? Am I concerned more for success in society than for God's approval? Am I too afraid I will fail? Am I in money trouble because of overspending, because of overstriving? Such things can suck the marrow out of life and leave us filled with nameless foreboding.

Questions like these need to be asked often, because every new day generates its own anxieties. We must therefore develop the skill of naming our anxieties to God. I'm under pressure today because _____ . This I can change, so by God's help I will. This I can't, so I will trust it to God.

This brings us to the main verb of the sentence, a verb occurring only one time in the New Testament. When the disciples brought the colt to Jesus, before He mounted, they *threw* their coats on the animal. Peter tells us this is what we are to do with our anxieties. We are to cast them on God.

How? Try writing on a sheet of paper the things that worry you and which you can't change. Then, burn the sheet to symbolize you're turning them over to God.

Why not? He cares *for you.* For YOU!

Chapter 4

Anger

Ours is an angry world.

Look at the faces of veterans pitching away their medals at the Capitol building. Listen to the jeers of Irishmen across barbed wire in the street.

It's everywhere, anger is. Maybe within arm's reach as you read this. Maybe within.

It can certainly be found in the church. Subdued for the most part, sometimes skillfully camouflaged, in any congregation of one hundred people you will find anger.

This should not seem strange. The Bible leaves us wondering whether Paul did not feel anger when he rebuked Elymas, the magician (Acts 13:8-11). The Bible describes the anger of Jesus (John 2:13-17). It even introduces us to the anger of God (Romans 2:1-11).

Anger is obviously a function of personality, both God's and man's. Take from God His ability to be angry, and you have only a benign grandfather, not the Ruler of the universe. Take from man his ability to be angry, and you have a Milquetoast.

Why then are we Christians so cagey about our anger?

Because our anger is usually of a selfish sort, not noble like Jesus' anger when He drove the greedy out of the Temple.

Human anger usually reflects the truth expressed in Christian doctrine: man is neither inherently good nor inherently evil. He is a good thing spoiled. That's what we mean when we say man is a ''fallen'' creature.

Anger, reflecting this reality, usually functions in a spoiled way. So we conceal what we know deep within is ignoble.

In fact, the denial of anger is a common way of dealing with it. Some Christians do such a skillful job that they thoroughly convince themselves that anger is nonexistent for them. But this leaves them hard pressed to explain the static in their relationships with others.

Sometimes we use anger as a weapon. Who has not seen a wife cow her husband by a hidden anger which the poor fellow knows about and fears to trigger? Husbands are not above using the same techniques on their wives.

Sometimes we use anger as a defense. When we don't want to hear something, our anger erupts like foam from a nozzle to extinguish truth. In this way, many an insight has been successfully resisted.

How can believers come to terms with anger? A renewal of Christian realism would help. The New Testament sees human nature without cosmetics. Jesus said the heart generates evil (Mark 7:20-23). Paul exhorted believers to ''put off the lower nature," thus acknowledging with candor that human nature has an even more radical need than forgiveness.

We could all recover the realism of what the New Testament says about human nature by reading it often with searching humility.

A renewal of Christian community would help, too. The Galatians ministered to one another in truthful and liberating ways. They blended truth with love.

Today, if a group of recovered addicts can surround a fellow human with sufficient concern to compel him to face his own rationalizations, thus starting him toward recovery, why can't Christians gently prod one another toward truth in a similar way? This is one thing Christian community means.

But our greatest need is to embrace again the deeper provision of Christ's redemption. Selfish anger is only one of many symptoms of sinful nature. The gospel calls us to bring this radical sinfulness to the cross (Galatians 5:24).

The gospel also calls us to surrender our inner being to the Holy Spirit who will make of it an orchard of Christ's graces (Galatians 5:22, 23).

Chapter 5

How to Deal with Your Doubts

It's tormenting enough to be racked by doubt, to wonder if God cares, if He can do anything for you in your straits.

But to add guilt to this torment, to feel that doubting is sinful and thus must be kept secret, seems more than any human can bear.

The truth is, doubt is the experience of aspiring saints. The smug know little of it.

There is no trace that fleshly Esau was ever tormented by doubt. Nor, so far as we know, was Samson, the playboy.

But Elijah was. And so were Jeremiah and Habakkuk and John the Baptist.

Jesus too had His rounds with doubt. No one before or since ever trusted the Father so implicitly. Yet from His cross He cried, "My God, my God, why. . .?

There are many expressions of doubt in the Psalms. More than forty of the one hundred fifty are called "psalms of complaint."

Psalm 77 is one of them.

This psalmist is in such distress he can't sleep at night. He holds God responsible for even this aspect of his trouble, since, to the Hebrew mind, God is ultimately responsible for every human situation.

The psalmist cries out in his anguish, "Has God forgotten to be gracious? Has he in anger shut up his compassion" (v. 9, RSV)?

The psalm must have begun as the solitary cry of one believer. But the Old Testament church discovered it, saw in it a cry common to many believers, and placed it in the Book. Now, all doubters may use it.

Not unbelievers.

The unbeliever is different. He does not want to believe in God. Answer his questions and he will reply with silence or more questions. Secretly, he sees God as his enemy.

Psalm 77 is for doubters.

The doubter wants to believe that God is his friend, but he doesn't see how things could be as they are if God *really* was his friend. He has faith but it is weak, qualified, strained.

How are we to deal with our doubts?

Frederick Robertson, great preacher of an earlier generation, had to deal with his. Sometimes they were black, almost overwhelming. What solution did he later recommend?

"I reply, obedience! Leave those thoughts [of doubt] for the present. Act — be merciful and gentle — honest. Force yourselves to abound in little services; try to do good to others; be true to the duty that you know. . . ."

Good advice. But there is a deeper word on the subject, and the psalmist speaks it.

26

"I will call to mind the deeds of the Lord," he says; "yea, I will remember thy wonders of old (v. 11, RSV).

Our doubts can easily preoccupy us, making us self-centered. The pslamist averted this peril by fixing his mind on the mighty acts of God in history. Principally, he meditated on God's deliverance of His people at the Red Sea.

We can go one better. For us, there are the mighty acts of God in Jesus. There is His life of love and healing. There is the wonder of Calvary. Above all, there is the mighty expression of power at Joseph's tomb. In the resurrection, even death was doomed.

To overcome your doubts, meditate long and often on God's mighty acts in history. Use such passages as Ephesians 1 and 2, and John 19. These will sharpen your focus, quicken your faith.

But be sure to meditate as often as you can in the presence of other believers. (Too much solitude is not good for doubters.) In worship, unite your shaky faith with the more robust faith of other worshipers.

This apparently is what the psalmist did.

Chapter 6

The Burden Sharer

We commonly think of Jesus Christ as the *burden bearer*. With prophetic foresight, for example, Isaiah said of the coming Messiah, "The Lord has laid on him the guilt of us all" (Isaiah 53:6, RSV). And, almost as if to elaborate this word, Peter said of the Messiah after His coming, "He himself bore our sins in his body on the tree" (I Peter 2:24, RSV). What good news: we are delivered from the burden of our sins by Christ who has borne them for us!

Not so commonly, however, do we think of Christ as the *burden sharer*. And yet, to His personal invitation to come to Him and find release from the galling weight of our sins, He adds an invitation to find rest in a shared servitude. He says, "Take my yoke upon you, . . . and you will find rest for your souls" (Matthew 11:29, RSV).

If the symbol for Christ the burden bearer is the cross, the symbol for Christ the burden sharer is the yoke. Only when each has a prominent place in our lives can we experience Christian living at its best.

The yoke, as every Palestinian knew, was a large timber, hand-hewn to fit the necks of two oxen. If it was poorly fashioned, the oxen were worn out by their labors. If it fit well, they could pull a large load without undue strain. When Jesus said, "My yoke is good to bear, my load is light" (Matthew 11:30, *NEB*), He meant, My yoke is fashioned to fit you.

Men do wear yokes that do not fit. There is evidence of this fact in the chapter that contains this invitation. The cities of Chorazin, Bethsaida, and Capernaum had seen Christ's mighty works in their streets but had rejected His appeal. It is an obviously irrational rejection of greatness. How does one explain this? The rejecters must have been under a hidden yoke they did not recognize and could not shake, an ill-fitting collar of pride.

Pride is the root of all sin and is the universal experience of men. Those who rejected Christ's works did so because they did not want to bow to His claims. It is the nature of pride to want to go it alone, to remain independent from God. Behind a hundred masks — from smug piety to bold impiety — pride secretly strives to be God. Over the prideful cities, Jesus could do no more than pronounce judgment — a horrible searing judgment worse than Sodom ever knew.

Pride is still the ill-fitting yoke that keeps men from Christ's best, and their own. We seldom detect it in ourselves because it is to our advantage to keep it hidden. But the symptoms of its presence gives us away. The spiritually proud are worn out by the burdens of life. God resists the proud.

Jesus' invitation is to lay off this chafing yoke and enter with Him into a companionship that suits our natures. He shares with us the burdens that make men great — burdens over the hurts of humanity. And best of all, He does not send us to our labors, but, under the symbol of a yoke, He invites us to share with Him life's labors. He is the burden-sharing Christ.

"Bend your necks to my yoke," He says, "and learn from me" (Matthew 11:29, *NEB*). It is a gracious invitation, but entirely without coercion. If we accept it, we accept the joy of His companionship in the common tasks of life. If we refuse, we do so only to bend our necks to some ill-fitting yoke.

We are members of a proud generation. The chafe on the spirit of modern man is evidence of this fact. But, into the prideful arena of contemporary life, the call of Christ sounds clearly. "Come to me . . ." and "bend yoar necks to my yoke" *(NEB)*.

Chapter 7

Art and Verna and the Cross

I met Art and his wife, Verna, in a city hospital where a mangled leg had put him. Our friendship grew until the three of us talked easily of Christ and His claims.

Meanwhile, a Christian nurse gave them a Bible, and they started to read it. They found it a strange and haunting book.

I didn't realize how strange until one day Verna asked, "This man Jesus — did He die and come to life four times?" She had read straight through the four Gospels and had come upon the same facts about His death at the end of each.

If she had read further, she would have found the cross profiled in the Acts, the New Testament letters, and even foreshadowed in the Old Testament.

As Suzanne de Dietrich says, "From the first page of Genesis to the last page of Revelation, everything that happens points towards this cross, and likewise everything arises from it."

What a paradox, that God's love should be discerned in a Roman execution. Nevertheless, as Donald Baillie puts it, "The most remarkable fact

31

in the whole history of religious thought is this: that when the early Christians looked back and pondered on this dreadful thing that had happened, it made them think of the redeeming love of God.''

There is more than love displayed on Golgotha's cross, however. God's eternal judgment on man's sin is evident as well.

''The cross,'' says J. S. Whale, ''is the place where sinful men must come nearest to understanding what sin must mean to the holy love of God.'' The modern mind, uneasy in its use of such words as *sin* and *holiness,* has trouble here.

Verna did not. The cross had given her a glimpse of her own self-will against God, showing its enormity. She had never known herself so deeply as she did in the light of the cross.

Seeing God's love and her own rebelliousness mirrored in the same event moved her to tears. Art was less emotional but deeply affected.

Some might say the word of the cross was no more than a clever device to generate guilt feeling. J. S. Whale, with a better grasp of it all, says, ''The evil that I have done and the evil that I have set afloat in the lives now far beyond my reach or control is objective fact for ever.''

Anyone who takes the cross seriously sees that his own sins have disturbed the universe in a way he can never correct. His penitence and restitution, however urgently offered, are never more than token efforts at righting wrongs. If it is to be done thoroughly, God himself must do it, and the cross is His way.

Art and Verna, to a degree, sensed all this.

Nevertheless, their story did not have a happy-ever-after ending. Verna said, "No," with tears and tight little movements of her head. Art said it with more control.

Even so, the cross has left its mark. In the deepest redoubts of their beings, wherever they are, they know they are the objects of God's love. They will never again be at ease in their rebellion.

Verna (there are Vernas wherever people gather), Christ died only once, but it was for you. Do you see that your self-will is bondage and God's love is freedom?

Art (there are Arts in every county across the nation), the cross is at the heart of the gospel because there God's love is seen as greater than your wrongs, and His judgment on your sin is somehow thorough enough to permit you a new start in life.

Chapter 8

Grow in Grace Now!

Ever since Christ came into the world, every moment has become an urgent moment, and God's call to men is always a call to respond in obedience *now*.

"Behold, now is the acceptable time; behold, now is the day of salvation" (II Corinthians 6:2, RSV). This is so for the person outside Christ. But it is also true for the person in Christ who needs to grow in the grace and knowledge of our Lord and Saviour Jesus Christ.

If you are in the latter class, feeling vaguely at a standstill and wanting a new spirit of growth to be set off in your life, here's a checklist of three areas in which growth *now* may be possible.

1. Grow in Christian witness

I haven't forgotten the thirteen-year-old boy who came to our home with literature to sell and a speech to make. I invited him in, but the speech hadn't gone far before the doorbell rang again and an anxious father peered in. They were Jehovah's

34

Witnesses working the street.

One thing the Jehovah's Witnesses teach us is that a person is never fully committed to his faith until he is willing to bear open witness to it.

But why learn it from Jehovah's Witnesses? The Acts of the Apostles is a running narrative of Christian witness. "We cannot help but speak" seems to be the confession shared by that early Christian company.

Speaking up is at the center of the Christian witness. The gospel is more than mere words, but it is never less. It may be enhanced by the example of a good life, but a good life by itself will never tell the world that "Christ died for our sins in accordance with the scriptures, that he was buried, that he was raised on the third day in accordance with the scriptures" (I Corinthians 15:3, 4, RSV). That requires a voice.

"If on your lips is the confession, 'Jesus is Lord,' " Paul wrote to the Romans, ". . . then you will find salvation" (10:9, *NEB)*. This fragment from one of the earliest creeds makes clear that back then a convert not only believed in his heart that Christ had been raised from the dead, he also confessed with his lips the reality of his lordship.

Back then? Why not now?

Ask God to bring into your life in the next twenty-four hours someone whom you can tell that Jesus is Lord. Then, prayerfully watch for the opportunity and take it when it comes. Better still, join one of the small groups who make community evangelism a weekly part of their Christian discipleship. It will scare you, but you'll grow.

2. Grow in Christian service

Shortly after his conversion Jim Vaus, notorious wiretapper of the late forties, mowed his neighbor's lawn. It was no calculated opener for evangelism, only a spontaneous overflow of a newfound love, though it in fact opened the way for later witness.

God puts such things as lawns into all our lives if we can focus closely enough to see them.

An industrial editor wrote, "One trouble with professional religionists . . . is that they are concerned chiefly with expressing love wholesale. They fail to see that . . . retailing is more important, because it delivers the product where it is used." Christian service is God's love retailed.

If you feel that growth is lagging because you are deficient in service to others, here are four suggestions to stimulate your spiritual growth glands.

First, start near you. Your home is always headquarters for your field of service.

Second, start small. Don't wait to serve until you can do something dramatic. Jesus said, "He that is faithful in that which is least is faithful also in much" (Luke 16:10).

Third, use your imagination. Mary poured her perfume over Jesus' feet.

Fourth, "whatever you do, in word or deed, do everything in the name of the Lord Jesus" (Colossians 3:17, RSV).

3. Grow in Christian devotion

Christians who are active in witness and service get hungry for food to restore spent energies. When they do, the Bible is always the source of nourishment to which they turn.

Allan Richardson writes, "If God speaks to men through the Church, that is because the Church is the place where the Bible is read, or it is the community which listens to the public reading of the Bible. If God speaks to men through the sacraments, that is because they are sacraments of the Bible-drama. If God speaks to men in the sermon, that is because the Bible is preached.

"If God speaks to men in prayer, that is because the prayer is the prayer of the Bible. And if God speaks to men through nature, or through things which are lovely and characters which are noble, that is because they have learnt from the Bible the accents of his voice."

You may feel undernourished because your experience with the Bible is too bland. If so, try this change:

Don't just read the Bible with your eyes; interact with it at every level of your being. (Passive readers of any book don't get much good from their reading.) As you read, ask the Bible questions. Write insights down. Turn into a prayer whatever the Bible says to you. Even an infant, you may have noticed, becomes actively involved in the process of his feeding.

If you have read this far, you must already have pinpointed areas in which you need to grow. You may be a tongue-tied Christian or one whose service to humanity is largely in the realm of theory or one who feels chronically malnourished.

But knowing this will not change anything unless you set out to change. In fact, if you lay these suggestions aside without doing something resolute about them, before an hour passes the concern to change will wane. God's time is *now*.

Strong words? The Bible is full of strong words. Too urgent? How can they be when they invite wholehearted response to one who has died in our behalf?

Chapter 9

Getting Back into the Word

A high school freshman put her *Reach Out* paraphrase of the New Testament into my hands two weeks ago. I thumbed its pages and discovered they were generously marked in vivid blue ink — here a verse underlined, there a word boxed.

I've heard members of this new generation of Christians speak often of "getting into the Word." Judging by the appearance of one of their New Testaments, they not only talk about it, they do it.

It makes me want to speak to the older generation of Christians, those of us who have more than a decade of time to our credit and who have come to feel comfortable in the category.

I've discovered that if my daily use of the Bible isn't periodically revitalized I'm in trouble. A dull routine sets in which may easily slip into no more than a fading memory.

My freshman friend is "getting into the Word." And you? Do you ever feel the need to get *back* into the Word?

If so, here are some ideas to ponder. They may help you get a fresh view of what the Bible is and what it is for, and they may offer some basic requirements for really getting into it.

First, think of the Bible as the book in which God addresses you personally.

You may have thought of the Bible as an encounter with chapter and verse numbers, archaic words, and funny-sounding names like Mahershalalhashbaz.

If so, no wonder your ardor has cooled. When looked at this way, the Bible can become as forbidding to the average man as an old set of *Hastings' Encyclopedia of Religion and Ethics.* Hastings' is full of valuable information, but who turns to it for daily sustenance?

You'll be better off to think of the Bible as the narrative of God's dealings with men in history. Chapters and verses are helpful markers. The Mahershalalhashbazes are part of the story. But the leading actor is God, and since He is the living God, He who spoke then speaks now.

In a word, you have a right to come to your daily Bible reading expecting an encounter with the living God. When you do, the Bible cannot remain dull to you.

Second, when you read your Bible, expect God to address you in judgment as well as mercy.

"We dismiss the Bible," says Robert McAfee Brown, "not because it is out-of-date but because it is much too up-to-date; it describes far too accurately who we are and where we have gone wrong."

It may seem contradictory to you for a Christian to read the Bible to learn where he has gone wrong. Is he not a child of God, fully forgiven, and "in Christ"?

Though all this is true, it is also true that God deals with His children much as Jesus dealt with His disciples. He chided them for unbelief, admonished them not to become hosts to the Pharisaic spirit, and was indignant with them when they wanted to turn the children away from Him.

If we expect from the Bible only words of assurance, we will experience only half its ministry to us. Expecting only this may even cause us to come to it in smugness, a sure way to dampen our interest. But if we come expecting reproof and correction as well, we will experience its whole ministry and begin to know the full range of the love of God. Every Christian who comes in this frame of mind begins to experience the Bible as a precious — though often probing — book.

Third, reexamine the details of your daily experience with the Bible.

Details always matter for those who want to do things well. In photography, for example, attention to detail separates the professional from the amateur.

It is so in reading the Bible. If you put in time with small benefits, it may be that you are being careless about small but important details.

Do you have a place where you go regularly to commune with God through the Scriptures? One college student refused to be thwarted by crowded conditions. He finally found quietness in a furnace room.

Whenever possible you should go to the same place every day; and in our kind of world, finding that place may take creative searching. But if the college student could do it, why not you?

Do you have a time you guard jealously — preferably the same time each day and during the freshest part of the day? A young woman could not make sense of her Bible early in the morning. So she started her day with a short prayer of commitment and then halved her lunch hour, taking thirty minutes for lunch and thirty minutes for her Bible.

Read systematically. Finish one book of the Bible before beginning another. Alternate between Old and New Testaments, keeping the stronger emphasis on the New without neglecting the Old. Ask your minister for a schedule to follow so you can read the Bible through in a year.

When it comes to daily Bible reading, system does matter. Stick with one plan until you find a better one. Dabbling in the Bible is a sure way to quench your interest.

Do you use techniques to make yourself interact with what you read? One Bible lover I know overprints. He buys editions with tough paper, and when he comes to a passage that seems to offer help, he prints over the words letter by letter as if he were writing the words himself. He says it slows him down and makes him think.

There are many ways to intensify attention: underlining, outlining, paraphrasing, note-taking. One of these must be suited to your needs. Find it and use it diligently until you get to the state where you never feel comfortable reading the Bible without a pencil in your hand.

All sorts of new Christians are "getting into the Word" these days. And not a few long-standing Christians who have gone through barren years are "getting *back* into the Word."

This is one phase in a quiet Christian renewal affecting every corner of the continent. Young and old alike are getting caught up in it. If the Holy Spirit breathes desire into your heart to get back into the Word, today is the day to begin.

Chapter 10

Get High, Man!

At the 9,000-foot level of the Sangre de Cristo Mountains here in Colorado, a little exertion makes you puff. At the 12,000-foot level, climb a while and you begin to suck air to the bottom of your lungs. But you don't mind puffing up a mountain trail when every gain in elevation broadens your view of the Wet Mountain Valley below and the string of hazy mountains on the horizon beyond.

The climb has brought a spiritual quickening that takes me by surprise. Sitting on a conglomerate rock (breathing normally now) I sense God's nearness, and with cleansed vision see that the world stretched out below is His world. "The earth is the Lord's and the fulness thereof. . . ," I hear in my memory. I shall return renewed to Horn Creek Lodge nearby.

It must be no accident that Moses saw the glory of God on Mount Sinai and later the splendor of the promised land from Mount Nebo. It is no coincidence that Abraham faced the supreme test of obedience to God on Mount Moriah and that

Elijah, in the name of Jehovah, broke Baal's pagan control over Israel on Mount Carmel.

Nor is it surprising that mountains played so large a place in Jesus' life. He was tempted on a mountain, He taught His followers on a mountain, and was transfigured before them on a mountain. Repeatedly, He sought the solitude of a mountain to commune with His Father.

Here on the slopes of Mount Horn I begin to see. Modern life often lacks the elevation the human spirit must have to survive. We have a lowlander's mentality, most of us, whether we live in the city or the country. At best we live on rolling prairies, with a little religion, a little prayer; at worst, with incessant TV, trite reading, and a shabby stream of consciousness, we live at the oozy edges of a slough. We moderns need periodically to get up where life's vision is cleansed. We need, to borrow an expression, to get high.

But not high as the hippies do northeast of here in the surging university city of Boulder. They have made this city a summer gathering place. On its streets, their clothes sport a profusion of patches, their long hair often frames granny glasses; and you will find them in pairs in any supermarket buying a bit of food for their next meal.

Hippies also feel that modern man is a lowlander. They feel it with a despair etched into their doleful faces. For them, the past is unimportant, the future hopeless, and the present in a plastic culture so meaningless that you can only get above it with "grass" or "acid."

Their solution is to get high, but their method is so different from hiking on a mountain. There's no effort, no stretching of muscles, only a dreary telling of the world to go away. It's all so sad when you see in their faces unrealized possibilities being destroyed. And in their faces too is an unspoken word to jaded people in the straight world.

What I begin to see here amidst blue spruce and ponderosa pine is that mountain hiking has a spiritual equivalent. However level the ground where we live, we must find ways regularly to gain spiritual elevation if we are to survive in a chaotic world. Otherwise, our state will be little different from that of the hippies, except for the drugs. We will become the straight world's casualties.

How can we get elevation in a cluttered world? A college student, determined to keep his life fresh in spite of the pressures, found an unused attic room and went there daily, New Testament in hand, for prayer. A well-known Christian leader pushed his rising time back from six to five to four. He was determined to be alone with God before the day's tasks confronted him.

It's not easy, but neither is climbing on a mountain. The apartment dweller may need to walk to a nearby cemetery or go to the altar of a quiet church. The farmer may have to slip away to an unused shed. We may have to find our mountains in unexpected places, or even make them.

Gaining spiritual elevaton takes discipline, but the view is worth it. And when one comes away from a high moment with God, there's new energy for the tasks on the plains below.

Chapter 11

Vacations Can Be Spiritual

He was an expert on the Bible. He had
discussed it, taught it, even published on its great
themes. Yet, in 1913, when illness struck him, his
legacy of knowledge didn't help much.

H. Wheeler Robinson, late Bible scholar whose
excellence is widely recognized to the present,
found himself asking, in his illness, why the
teachings of "evangelical" Christianity seemed to
fail him.

In his distress, a figure formed in his mind. He
saw a great balloon, powerful enough to lift a ton
and dangling a rope from its underside. The
balloon could lift him, he knew, if only he could
grasp the rope. But he didn't have the strength.

His lack was in "his relative neglect," he later
wrote, "of those conceptions of the Holy Spirit in
which the New Testament is so rich." Out of this
discovery came his book, *The Christian Experience
of the Holy Spirit.*

Most Christians form an image in their minds
when the Holy Spirit is mentioned. If it is not that
of a great balloon, it is something else less
mechanical, perhaps, or more biblical.

Recently, a small knot of Christian youth was asked, "What do you think of when the Holy Spirit is mentioned?"

"I think of a flickering flame," one said, cupping his hands.

Another responded, "I think of the tongues-of-fire carving on the pulpit at church."

After a long pause a third said, "I think of a *vague* force."

They're good answers. Even so, the memory of H. Wheeler Robinson's experience lingers as they're listed. Are they only theoretical answers, or are they rooted in the personal experience of the Holy Spirit?

We ask the same question of ourselves when matters regarding the Holy Spirit arise. For us, is He like a great balloon, dangling a rope which in our neediest moments we can't get hold of? Is He only a *vague* force?

Or is He a living person to be obeyed and communed with? Is He the Spirit of Christ, dwelling in us, making His presence known in teaching, guidance, and reproof?

We may not know for sure until severe illness overtakes us, setting us aside as it did H. Wheeler Robinson.

But there are better times to face the question. Like vacation time. Anyone who wishes can turn into a time of discovery the two or three weeks of the year when phones stop jangling and schedules stop pressing. Whether he heads for the lake or the mountains or stays at home, he can do so.

It takes only a Bible, a concordance, and a notebook. It will also take an hour a day for study

49

— preferably in the freshness of the morning and recurring times of meditation during the day.

The Gospel of Luke is an excellent area to work in. It is a Gospel of the Spirit. The concordance will mark out the richest passages. The notebook will preserve thoughts and insights. And the times of meditation will transform theory into reality.

I know one person who found a vacation like this to be as spiritually enriching as a Bible conference. There was time for play in the out-of-doors. There was time for travel and socializing. But the time that did the most good was the time of study and meditation.

He returned to his work, he reports, in the power of the Holy Spirit.

Chapter 12

Another Counselor

If you're going to build a house, you can talk to an architect. If you're going abroad, you look up a travel agent. If you're going to college, you get in touch with a high school counselor.

Ours is the age of counselors. We're just not up to the complexities of modern life on our own.

Yet, we Christians are in danger of neglecting the greatest counselor of all, the Holy Spirit.

"And I will pray the Father," Jesus promised, "and he will give you another Counselor, to be with you for ever" (John 14:16, RSV).

Literally, Jesus called the Holy Spirit a *Paraclete* at least four times (14:16, 26; 15:26; 16:7).

The King James Version translates the word "Comforter." But from its earlier meaning of "strengthener," this has come to mean to us something more like "consoler." Consoling is only a part of what the *Paraclete* does.

Other translations use terms like "helper," which is essentially correct but not specific enough.

Taken in its root meaning, a *Paraclete* is one

who stands at our side cheering us on; or one we may summon for aid.

Today, think of a *Paraclete* as a track man's coach in a hard race, or a client's lawyer in a tough problem. He's available, knows what's needed, and thus gives help and comfort.

What did Jesus mean by referring to Him as "another" counselor.

If a man suggests to his wife a plan for their vacation and she replies, "I have another idea," she means "different," or maybe "opposite."

But if a man and his wife are coming to the toll road exit and are pooling their resources and he says, "I have a dollar bill," to which she replies, "I have another," she means "duplicate."

Jesus had been a *Paraclete* to His disciples. By His promise of another counselor He meant that the Holy Spirit would provide not a different but a duplicate ministry in their lives.

For example, the Spirit would bring to their remembrance all things that Jesus himself had said to them. (When Christians come alive to the Holy Spirit, they come alive to the Scriptures, too.)

The Spirit duplicates Jesus' counseling ministry all right. But what Jesus did locally, the Holy Spirit does universally. This means for believers in Hong Kong and Brazil at the same time.

Is this merely a wonderful idea? "The watchword of the men who penned the New Testament," wrote James Denney, "was not *believe* in the Holy Ghost, but *receive ye* the Holy Ghost."

He is more than a doctrine to be understood; He is a person to be experienced. He is the

Paraclete sent from the Father to be with us forever.

In the fury of our times, there's a quiet revolution going on. The Holy Spirit leads, making Jesus real to new believers and old ones, too.

If you want to get in on it, expose yourself daily for two weeks to Jesus' words about the *Paraclete*. Begin to open your life up to Him, answering His call to complete obedience. As you do, expect the Counselor to make His presence and leadership felt.

Become a part of God's revolutionary force in the world.

Chapter 13

The Holy Spirit Is No "Clown"

"Some people think of the Holy Spirit as a sort of clown of the Trinity," my friend's voice said at the other end of the line.

He had been talking with a group of six or so who are trying to start the whole Christian enterprise with a clean slate.

What had impressed him most about the group was their novel way of talking about the Holy Spirit. Hence, his daring analogy, "the clown of the Trinity."

I asked him for an explanation. "Well," he said, "these people think of God the Father as sort of old and stodgy and pretty authoritative. God the Son belongs to a time in history remote from ours.

"But, God the Spirit," he went on, "is the exciting person of the Trinity. He does all sorts of startling and colorful things. You never know what might happen."

My friend's analogy is a bit daring, I'll admit. But in times of religious upheaval like ours, the Holy Spirit is bound to come in for animated discussion.

And those who develop notions of the Spirit

discordant with what we learn of Him through the Scriptures are bound to go astray. They may even come to think of Him as religion's answer to the world's craving for entertainment.

We should review fundamentals on the Holy Spirit periodically. What guidance does the New Testament give us?

For one thing, it makes clear that the Holy Spirit of God is always a *personal presence.*

Personal? Read the Acts of the Apostles and place an *S* beside every reference to the Holy Spirit. Then spend a few days meditating on these references.

You'll come across Peter's no-nonsense rebuke of Ananias, charging him with lying to the Holy Spirit. Does one take a clown seriously enough to lie to him? Lying is a serious moral offense because it is a deception perpetrated by one real person against another.

You'll come across Philip's conversation with the Ethiopian eunuch after being instructed by the Spirit to climb into the eunuch's chariot. Doesn't this sound like the responsible ordering of one person's life by another?

My friend remarked that the group he had been in touch with associated the Holy Spirit with excitement. There can be no doubt He does affect human feelings, but not as a roller coaster does, nor as pot, nor even as Pepsi on a steamy day. He affects them as one august person affects another, stirring joy or confidence or sorrow. The Spirit is always a *personal presence.*

Moreover, we are told in the Scriptures that the Holy Spirit is the *Spirit of Christ.*

Paul the Apostle speaks of "the Spirit of Jesus Christ" or "the Spirit of Christ" or "the Spirit of God's Son" (Philippians 1:19; Romans 8:9, 14; Galatians 4:6). He even goes so far as to say "the Lord is the Spirit" (II Corinthians 3:17), not thus confusing their separate identities but highlighting their common purpose.

In view of these expressions, we can assume that the Holy Spirit will prompt in us only what is consistent with the character of Christ. The fruits of the Spirit, in fact, are the graces of Christ.

We can assume, conversely, that whatever in our conduct does not square with the character of Christ (however colorful it may make us seem) cannot be attributed to the Holy Spirit. As one man, wise in the ways of the Spirit, used to say, "We will always act like the spirit we are possessed with."

Clowns belong to an unreal world, a world contrived for temporary escape and frivolity.

The Holy Spirit *is no clown*. He belongs to the real world, the world created for the glory of God. It is a real world in which a real God seeks to confront real people. When the Holy Spirit is honored, He raises more than merriment. He generates *real* joy.

Chapter 14

The Battle of the Christian Heart

To take the Spirit-controlled life seriously, we must also be serious about life dominated by the flesh.

These are options before every Christian, as Romans 8 and Galatians 5:16 — 6:10 make clear.

What is the *flesh?* The Apostle Paul uses the term in a wide variety of ways. Let's look at three.

Flesh sometimes refers to human nature in terms of its weakness. In Paul's own testimony to the resurrected life, he says, ''The life I now live *in the flesh* I live by faith in the Son of God'' (Galatians 2:20, RSV).

He often bears witness that the Christian life can be one of triumph. But not without moment-by-moment trust in Jesus Christ, because even the most dedicated Christian life is lived out in the sphere of human weakness.

Should we acknowledge this? We had better. Look at any Christian congregation. What about the periodic depressions? The problems of senility? And many others. Good Christians are often involved.

Flesh sometimes refers to human nature as vulnerable to sin. The Galatians were warned, "Do not use your freedom as an opportunity for the flesh" (5:13, RSV). That is, do not let your flesh give sin a foothold.

Flesh in this sense, says William Barclay, can be thought of as a bridgehead, that feature of fallen human nature which makes it subject to attack from behind the lines.

Flesh sometimes refers to human nature not as merely weak or vulnerable but as sinful. The "works of the flesh" (Galatians 5:19-21) are sins which fallen human nature, on its own, will inevitably generate.

There are eighteen sins in St. Paul's partial list, and these can be divided into four classes.

There are sensual sins: immorality (fornication), uncleanness (sensuality as it affects the inner state of things), licentiousness (wanton disregard for public decency).

There are religious sins: idolatry, witchcraft.

There are interpersonal sins: enmity (hidden feelings of unbrotherliness), strife, jealousy (self-assertive rivalry), anger, selfishness, dissension (open hostility), party spirit (open breach of relationships), envy (desire to deprive another of what he has), murder (hate which would take another's life).

There are vulgar sins: drunkenness and carousing.

Spirit-controlled living is only possible if we are willing to look at these darker capabilities of human nature.

When we do, we first see that *flesh* as sinful human nature cannot be educated or disciplined into good behavior. It can only be ruthlessly crucified (Galatians 5:24).

We see, moreover, that human nature, because of its weakness and vulnerability to sin, must be brought, by the aid of the mighty Spirit of God, into a life-style marked by discipline.

This includes systematic instruction (which is what the Galatian letter is), the worship and fellowship of the Christian community (5:25 — 6:9), and the daily practice of sowing in the field of the Spirit rather than in the field of the flesh (6:7-9).

In a word, the Spirit-controlled life is no accident. It is, moreover, not a solo performance, but a life lived in concert with other believers.

It is not, however, a life of introspective fear. Facing the issues of carnal conflict requires introspection. Living a disciplined life will, too. But introspection is not the last word.

The last word of the Spirit-controlled life is service. "So then, as we have opportunity, let us do good to all men, and especially to those who are of the household of faith" (6:10, RSV).

Chapter 15

Three Persons You Could Be

If you have been exposed to the gospel — by radio, through Inter-varsity, over a lifetime of churchgoing — there are three options before you. You could become a natural man, a spiritual man, or a carnal man. Let's look.

The natural man (I Corinthians 2:14). When it comes to the gospel, this man draws a blank. He's the sort who at a Billy Graham Crusade listens for a few minutes and then walks out mumbling. Or who watches the neighbor's family load up for church and waves amiably but thinks how foolish it all is.

Today we would call him "physical." His ability to experience God has been deadened by disuse and abuse. He has disqualified himself for God's truth by choosing the base in life.

He is like a telephone with the wires cut. The equipment looks normal, but messages don't get through. He "refuses what belongs to the Spirit of God; it is folly to him; he cannot grasp it" (NEB).

The spiritual man (I Corinthians 2:15). We easily caricature this person. We call him "spiritual" because of his language, voice inflections, gestures, attire, even his prejudices. Sometimes we do it sincerely, sometimes to escape obligation.

But, whether Salvationist or Episcopalian, he is simply a person possessed by God's Spirit. His church tradition, his educational standing, even his geographical background show. But these are incidental — expressions of God's penchant for variety. Always at the center, God's Holy Spirit dominates.

Is he characterized by poise? Not always. Paul says, "I came before you weak, nervous, and shaking with fear" (2:3, *NEB*). But he adds that his preaching carried "conviction by spiritual power" (2:4, *NEB*). He is not so much poised as possessed.

The spiritual man is a taught man. The Corinthians thought of spiritual stature in terms of ecstasy. Here they are asked to think of it in terms of education. The Holy Spirit himself, through apostles and Scripture, is the teacher (2:6-13).

The spiritual man has spiritual insight into life. "A man gifted with the Spirit can judge the worth of everything" (2:15, *NEB*). He sees through lust for power, striving for success, and other motives common in the world. It is a perilous ability, slipping easily into arrogance, but he is saved as he remembers it is a gift from the mind of Christ (2:16).

The carnal man (I Corinthians 3:1-4). This person is in the church, but not far. He's not the natural man, for he has received some measure of the Spirit. He's not the spiritual man, for he lacks the maturity the Spirit fosters. He's in the church nursery, an infant in Christ.

His carnality shows by a childish delight in taking sides. He is divisive. He may get a crush on Paul and dislike Apollos. Or vice versa. Even when he is clever enough to hide it, his divisiveness is at work.

Moreover, in his inner life he has never risen above the childish impulses of jealousy and strife. The success of others clouds his mind. He is a person of periodic, wrenching inner turmoil, however placid his face. And all because he has never yielded his inner being to the Holy Spirit's control and thus has not grown up in the Lord.

The three persons are in every congregation. The three possibilities are in every one of us. How does one become the spiritual man?

The key is in God's Spirit — the living presence of God searching, quickening, exhorting, teaching, wherever the gospel is heard. Permit Him to put His finger on whatever is childish in your life. Confess these things to God and to trusted Christians. Enlist prayers to be able to see clearly and renounce utterly. All the while, yield yourself to the sovereign Spirit's power.

In a word, to be the natural man, one must simply repeatedly say, "No." To be the spiritual man one must decisively and repeatedly say, "Yes." To be the carnal man, one need only continue to say, "Maybe."

Chapter 16

Helps Toward the Spirit-filled Life

We hear about it and have vague longings for it. Sometimes we misunderstand or fear it. But, in spite of our conflicting feelings, it is a level of life to which God calls every believer. It is the Spirit-filled life. Here's a simple outline to guide you in your spiritual progress:

I. Every true believer in Jesus Christ has the Holy Spirit in him.

    A. The believer has been given a new quality of life — washing and regeneration by the Spirit, Paul calls it (Titus 3:5). This is also called new birth, or birth by the Spirit (John 3:5).

    B. It was when they were converted to Christ that the Galatian Christians received the Holy Spirit (Galatians 3:1-3.) The same is true now.

II. But every new Christian soon discovers that his inner life is torn by conflict — sometimes more raging than it was before his conversion.

    A. Paul calls this the battle between the "flesh" — the lower nature, the old, self-centered life — and God's Holy Spirit (Galatians 5:17).

    B. James refers to a similar state of affairs, a battle between faith and doubt, as double-mindedness (James 1:6-8).

    C. The confessing Christian, then, experiences inner impulses that baffle and shame him. When they break out into conduct, they fill him with remorse. They are cataloged as the "works of the flesh" (Galatians 5:19-21).

III. He may be tempted to ignore, or hide from others, this unpleasant side of his life. Sometimes he even may succeed in hiding it from himself.

    A. He is hard pressed then to understand the conflict within and the recurrent conflicts between himself and others (James 3:13 — 4:3).

    B. Such Christians, always halfway sorry, always inwardly perplexed, and always lacking a rich sense of God's blessing, are called carnal Christians or babes in Christ (I Corinthians 3:1-3).

IV. To live life at the carnal level or to turn back to a fleshly way of living is a live but perilous option.

    A. It can result in a life of Christian mediocrity (I Corinthians 1:10-12).

    B. If life at this level becomes the norm again, spiritual death is threatened (Romans 8:6-8).

V. There is a level of Christian living far above this immature, carnal, tempestuous level.
   A. Paul exhorted the Ephesian Christians, who had received the Spirit (Acts 19:1-7), to be filled with the Spirit (Ephesians 5:18).
   B. He prayed that those who had God's Spirit in them would be "strengthened with might by his Spirit in the inner man" (Ephesians 3:16).
VI. This call to a higher level of Christian living requires certain responses.
   A. Faith that God wants the believer to know in rich measure the Holy Spirit's control and leadership (Luke 11:9-13).
   B. Honesty with God in identifying and taking sides against the fleshly responses to life that struggle for expression and dominance. Paul speaks of crucifying the flesh — ruthlessly bringing the lower nature to Christ's cross and identifying it there with Christ's death (Galatians 5:24). He also speaks of living the crucified life (Galatians 2:20).
   C. Obedience to the Holy Spirit. In the Spirit-filled life, there is no substitute for obedience (Acts 5:32). No amount of ecstasy, no recourse to special gifts can take its place.
VII. When, by faith, the believer begins to live the Spirit-filled life, certain evidences will witness to the fact.
   A. Jesus will become more real and

personal than He has ever been (John 14:15-21; 16:12-15). (The Spirit's instrument for making Him real is the Scriptures.)

B. The believer's desire will increase to fill his place in the body of Christ, the church, for fellowship (Acts 2:46), instruction (Acts 5:42), worship (Ephesians 6:18-20), support (Galatians 6:6), and service (Galatians 6:10).

C. The Holy Spirit will call him to a daily watchfulness to keep the inner life clean (I John 3:2, 3) and to deal frankly with sins that overcome him (I John 2:1, 2).

D. The Holy Spirit calls every believer to a three-way commitment:
— to God, giver of all grace (Romans 12:1-3)
— to Christ's church on earth (Romans 12:4-13)
— to the world Christ died to save (Romans 12:14 — 13:14).

And the call is in that order.

The key word is "faith." All God's gifts are given in response to faith. None are earned — not even by super-piety or super-consecration. Faith enables the believer to humbly face the truth about himself. Faith in God enables him to see and receive God's promises. It enables him to live day by day in confidence that "he which hath begun a good work in [him] will perform it until the day of Jesus Christ" (Philippians 1:6).

Chapter 17

Violence

When Cain brought his hoe smashing down on his brother Abel's head, the earth knew its first murder, and violence became a fact of human existence.

We moderns should understand the story, since violence is a part of our daily fare. Our children have seen cowboys by the score fall from their horses, dead, and we have watcted street riots and napalm attacks, close up and in color.

All this we have seen in the comfort of a family room which, more than once, may have witnessed its own kind of private violence.

It is the rare one among us who has not felt the stirrings of violent impulses. Demonstrators surging toward the ''fuzz'' at the intersection are driven by a hate compounded of misinformation and, perhaps, personal experience. The riot-jacketed police moving arm-in-arm toward them carry in their innards their own bitter memories of catcalls and baiting; they are impelled by more than a mere sense of duty. Meanwhile, viewers across the country take sides, with a slight rise in blood pressure. No wonder skulls are cracked.

Those who burn flags and those who fly them in reply appear by their conduct to be quite different, but the feelings of both are frighteningly similar. After Kent State more than one barber heard a half-shaven face say, "They should have shot a few more of them." Often, it was the face of a solid citizen. Sometimes of a churchgoer.

It is there — the ugly fact of violence — in every neighborhood. But who causes it? The establishment? The university? A corrupt public official?

Here's Cain. His murderous impulse can scarcely be charged to a bad neighborhood. Nor to an underprivileged home, since there were no other homes to measure privilege by. As the Bible tells the story, he was the first child of the human race, ready to worship and able to kill. John gives the cause. Cain "was of the evil one," he says, "and murdered his brother" (I John 3:12, RSV).

Before and after his murderous hoe fell, the Lord talked to Cain about the state of things. In a world where hoes have been replaced by high-velocity bullets, the Lord says the same things to us.

After worship, when the Lord saw Cain's angry face, He said to him: If you do well, you too will be accepted; if not, sin, like a wild beast, hides at the door of your heart waiting to spring. For the first time in the Bible, in an intensely personal setting, the word "sin" occurs.

Moreover, the Lord said to Cain, "You must master this beastly impulse," thus making him responsible for his conduct. No man can blame his

68

violence on a seedy neighborhood, as undesirable as such a neighborhood may be. Every man must accept responsibility for what's going on inside him and what he lets out.

After the murder, the Lord was there to confront Cain with a question: "Where is Abel your brother?" Nor would He be put off. Neither an ancient quip such as, "Am I the shepherd's shepherd?" nor a modern slogan such as "Every man must do his own thing" can get a person past God's social expectations. Cain was responsible for himself, and for his brother as well.

It should not surprise us that Cain was destined by the Lord to become a wanderer after his sin. He was to feel alienated from the ground, his home, his country, "Unrelieved guilt," someone more recently has said, "makes every man a moral exile."

But the Lord had a final word for Cain when Cain feared he would be murdered in revenge. "I will put a tattoo upon you," the Lord said, "and become your personal protector." God became the murderer's defender, a note of grace if ever there was one.

We ourselves may not be able to rid the world of violence, but we can make a contribution to a more stable future by enforcing the lessons of Cain in our own homes. Every child should be taught to acknowledge the darker impulses in his heart — jealousy, anger, vengefulness, and so forth. Beyond this, he should be helped to become responsible for controlling them. He should come to see as early as possible, moreover, that ours is a moral world in which no one is getting away with anything — in spite of appearances.

But this is not all. We have a saving word to give them, too. Controlling bad feelings can become little more than sitting on a powder keg, and this is scarcely salvation. We can teach our children that the Lord who marked Cain — saving him for later gospel opportunities? — can redeem them, cleansing their emotions and making love more normal than hate. It is the least they can expect from the power of Christ's death!

Chapter 18

Put Up Your Sword

Peter Schneider is a lawyer. He wrote a letter to the *New York Times* which began: "I wish to report that my brother has been murdered." The letter told of a respected brother, given to works of charity, who had been murdered in cold blood in his place of employment.

Scores of people responded to Schneider's letter. Most of them had themselves been objects of violent acts or knew someone who had.

The letter and responses highlighted once again a fact we are all painfully aware of: We live in a violence-prone society.

This may lead us to cry out in despair. It may push us to mount a campaign or to freeze in terror. But why not let it point up for us an overlooked fact in the church.

There are persons who profess faith in Christ but who struggle with urges to be violent. Sometimes these urges break out into conduct in more or less private ways. When they do, they create perplexity and remorse.

A young mother starts to correct her four-year-old daughter but ends up hurting her. She can't seem to help herself. She's in torment about it, but reading her Bible ever so earnestly doesn't help.

A man confesses secret impulses to choke his wife. He goes to church and sometimes fills the pulpit. He is ridden with guilt.

A rawboned teenager wants to hit his dad. As the boy talks of his feelings, he works the knuckles of his left hand with his right. He wants someone to pray with him.

Can people in such distress and bondage have any relationship at all to Christ?

Simon Peter was one of Jesus' inner circle. For three years he had been intimately exposed to the greatest man who ever lived and had come to share many of His convictions.

Yet, one night when a band of men came to take his leader, he suddenly produced a sword. Before anyone could stop him, he took a vicious swing at the head of the enemy nearest him. Fortunately, he only severed an ear.

This was an act of violence, yet each of the four gospel accounts reports it. It is not hushed up.

Of course, Peter had a reason for what he did. He was looking for the restoration of Israel. This meant to him political independence. Jesus was the man who could achieve it. Hence, Peter saw the situation as a showdown, and he was ready to do his part.

That's how we explain it. It's a plausible explanation, and it puts a slightly tarnished halo around Peter's head.

But why not a more basic explanation? Simon Peter was the sort of person who had in his nature the capacity to be violent. Our friend and brother, Simon Peter.

In a violent society, how can we help people who belong to Christ but who have moments when the impulse to draw a sword is almost beyond their resisting?

A young couple, married only a few weeks, turned up at their pastor's door. The wife explained that their times of playfulness sometimes began in laughter but ended for her in tears. She showed her bruises.

The husband admitted that in his boyhood physical aggression had been the order of the day. He had knocked both brothers around and more than once had nearly lit into his father. Now his wife was getting the treatment.

He had always excused himself for his urges to hurt others, but a time of confession brought him face to face with what he had never wanted to know about himself — other people didn't matter much.

By the time he had spoken in three directions — to God, to a respected member of his religious group, and to his wife — he saw the selfishness of his conduct with shocking clarity. In his case, this was enough. From that day on, his wife has never had to complain of abuse from him.

It is not always so simple. What of persons whose violent impulses are not quickly conquered? Young Christians in this plight need to know that they are loved and understood without being excused. In an atmosphere of genuine Christian concern they can pray and strive and hope until deliverance is a reality.

God's power to renew human nature is instantaneously available. But the understanding of this fact sometimes comes slowly, and deep conviction of need awaits its special moment. It was so with the young husband.

That is why a community of redeemed people who know the full range of their own potentialities for good and evil are needed to shepherd the violence-prone into the full light and power of the gospel.

"He breaks the power of cancelled sin, He sets the prisoner free." That's a line the early Methodists sang often. The hymnal page on which the song was printed was usually thumb-stained. The early Methodists believed it.

Let's revive the singing of that hymn. Let's revive confidence in its sentiments, too. This will create an atmosphere of faith in which people with hidden impulses to be violent can face and overcome their ugly, baffling impulses.

Chapter 19

How Many Worlds?

An earnest young face peered from the tube and said, "My world is different from yours." Matter-of-factly spoken, it was the first line of a commercial.

The line belongs to the youth generation. It is a cliché; and ad writers, detecting its currency, have picked it up and put it to good use.

In everyday speech, this cliché often has radical overtones. It means: There is no orderly world "out there," and so everyone, out of his subjective experiences, must create his own world. Consequently, there may be as many worlds as there are people.

The results of such thinking can be radical, too. The youth who says to his distraught parents, "My world is different from yours," may mean, "That's why I feel no shame for totally rejecting your values and treating you with contempt in the bargain." The cliché is also used to excuse lawbreaking, immorality, and even a sneering disdain for human life.

We who profess to be older and wiser can scarcely wag our fingers too self-righteously at this kind of thinking. We may not create worlds according to our own whims, but we have methods of dividing into segments the world that is.

Think of the worlds we have. There's the sports world, the business world, the entertainment world, the academic world, the medical world, and many others. These divisions may be more real to us than we care to admit. When a store manager says to a young minister, ''Get out of the church world and into the business world, and you'll see things differently,'' we nod in agreement. The implication may be that moral norms are different in the two worlds.

How different can one person's world be from another's? As different as a surveyor's is from an airline pilot's? They work in different spheres and use different skills, live in different communities, and move among different friends.

The differences are real, but are they as decisive as we have let them become? The surveyor and airline pilot share common fears and aspirations — fears of loneliness and death, and aspirations to be loved and to be holy. Chemically, moreover, the tears of the one can't be distinguished from the tears of the other. They live in different worlds, after a manner of speaking, but at the deeper levels of their existence they share a common world.

The Bible is very realistic about the dividedness of human life. Cain hated his brother and killed him. Jacob tricked his brother and fled him. The children of Ishmael and of Isaac were at enmity. The Northern Kingdom separated from the Southern Kingdom. And, in the early church, the Greek-speaking Christians charged ill treatment against the Hebrew-speaking Christians. The story of multiple worlds is there from beginning to end.

But this is not the decisive fact the Bible presents. The decisive fact, in two parts, is that God did not create the world divided, and He does not will for it to remain so. His world is a universe, not a multiverse, and His sweeping purpose is to bring back to unity what sin has so profoundly divided. His hidden purpose, Paul says, is "that the universe, all in heaven and on earth, might be brought into a unity in Christ" (Ephesians 1:10, *NEB*).

The church is His agent for the global aspect of this ministry, but one thing that holds us back is our own willingness to let the alien world define our terms. Its clichés so easily become ours. We can scarcely demonstrate the unity of all men in Christ if the young Christian can say uncritically to the older Christian, "My world is different from yours." That cliché needs examination in the light of Christ. Nor can we show this profound reconciliation while one older Christian holds himself slightly aloof from another because "People in the business world can't understand people in the university world." That cliché also needs examination in the light of Christ.

The world needs to see today that when God saves a surveyor and an airline pilot, their unity in Christ becomes more powerful than their differences in the world.

Chapter 20

The Gap Healer

In the church we sing, "We are not divided, all one body we, / One in hope and doctrine, one in charity." But in spite of our song, we are divided, precisely along the lines society is divided, and sometimes more deeply.

Look at some of the divisions in our culture.

There's the generation gap. "Millions of teens will run away from home this summer and crowd into big cities," predicts Paul Shanley, a priest to "street people" in Boston. We may blink at the figure, but we dare not shut our eyes to the gap between parents and children across a whole culture. Is it smaller in the church?

There's the work gap. The man in blue overalls on the scaffold has his private feelings about the man in the gray silk-and-wool suit on the street below. Between worker and boss there's little love lost. If each is a believer in Christ, does it make a difference?

There's the sex gap. The Women's Liberation Movement is bringing to light the hostility women feel toward men in what they consider a male-dominated world. Any psychiatrist, on the other hand, knows the crippling hostilities some men harbor toward "aggressive and domineering women." Can the church bridge this growing chasm?

There's the color gap. Twenty-five million blacks feel shut out of American society," says black evangelist Tom Skinner. Are they less shut out of the church?

Rifts like these are nothing new. In the world of the apostles, Jews and Gentiles scarcely tolerated one another, masters and slaves felt mutual disdain, men and women lived on different planes.

Into this divided world the gospel came to make a difference to the differences. It did not try to obliterate the differences, for example, by attempting to merge male and female into a unisex. A man is a man and a woman a woman. The gospel is realistic about life.

But the gospel says that in the light of Christ's reconciling work, all distinctions are paper thin. In the church, it is no longer the Jewish man nor the Gentile man but only the Christian man (Ephesians 2:13-16). That's the gospel's word to racial differences.

And to the other differences as well. Today, the painter and his boss should be able to sit side by side in the fellowship of the church, the teenager and his grandfather worship together at the communion rail. So male and female, black and white, rich and poor. The differences are there, but the gospel shows how superficial they are.

That is how sweeping the gospel really is.

"There is no such a thing as Jew and Greek, slave and freeman, male and female; for you are all one person in Christ Jesus" (Galatians 3:28, *NEB*). And that is the kind of reconciliation our chopped-up world needs, a reconciliation that reaches beneath all superficial distinctions to reveal to us our common humanity in Christ.

Chapter 21

Super City

"And I saw the holy city, new Jerusalem, coming down out of heaven from God, prepared as a bride adorned for her husband" (Revelation 21:2, RSV).

The city is neither Saint Louis nor Sodom. It doesn't belong to the ancient world buried beneath sand dunes nor to the modern world clouded with exhaust fumes. It isn't marked by human genius nor scarred by human depravity. Its splendor owes nothing to man, for it is not, in fact, the city of man; it is the city of God.

Men, wherever they have gone, have organized their environment. Their skills in social organization have come to a peak in the building of cities. Babylon, San Francisco, London, Atlanta — such highly developed communities have witnessed across history to the genius of their creators. Yet cities have fallen one by one, sacked by enemies, corrupted by inhabitants, or emptied by the uncertainties of history.

The Bible has a divided attitude toward cities. Jesus loved Jerusalem and wept over it in great tenderness, then pronounced destruction upon it. It was His city, the place of the patriarchs and prophets, and it had known great moments. But it distinguished itself for stoning the prophets. The city God had uniquely honored had swelled with pride and rejected His Son.

Yet the Bible begins its story of man in a garden and ends it in a city, "the new Jerusalem, coming down out of heaven from God" (Revelation 21:2, RSV). The vision of this city, given to John on Patmos, is rapturous, and the book of Revelation records it with power.

This last book of the Bible speaks throughout in what some have called cartoon language. A modern parallel is: The cartoonist today who wants to show the tension between Russia and Red China simply draws a bear being eyed menacingly by a red dragon. We know what these figures mean, and we get the message. Revelation is filled with verbal pictures — four-headed beasts, angels with vials, and cities like the new Jerusalem — from which we get a message too.

The message is that God himself will provide the perfect community for those who belong to Him. Paul calls it "the Jerusalem which is above" (Galatians 4:26), and "our commonwealth . . . in heaven" (Philippians 3:20, RSV). It is the city toward which Abraham was headed, "the city with firm foundations, whose architect and builder is God" (Hebrews 11:10, *NEB)*, the eternal dwelling place of God and His people.

Today the city of man is under a cloud — if not a hydrogen cloud, a cloud heavy with sulfur dioxide. It's a place of physical decay and human despair to many forgotten people, a hell without flames. Yet it keeps a proud silence about God and gropes only on the horizontal plane for solutions to its troubles.

Even so, Christ wept over a city ruled by such attitudes, and He healed persons in its dirty streets. Can we do less? In every city block are needs which compassionate Christians can meet, despair that can be relieved, boredom that can be replaced with meaning. In many decaying cities, small groups of Christians grapple with such problems.

But here's the paradox: We can serve with untiring compassion in the city of man only if we are convinced at every level of our beings that our true destination is the new Jerusalem, the city of God.

Chapter 22

Sounds from a River

You would not have called it a polluted river, but it was no sparkling mountain stream either. It twisted, snakelike, and fell rapidly toward the sea fifty miles below. Its brown waters were flanked by jungle growth. Its wildlife saw few humans, except, perhaps, those who came to its numerous fords.

It was a common river, but the crowds drawn to one of its fords this autumn season were uncommonly large. They had come to hear a mysterious wilderness dweller holding forth on its banks. Unsoftened by city life, he was making fearless demands on them. The field of force surrounding him was so powerful that the more disturbing his speeches, the larger the crowds became.

All sorts turned up. There were politicians of the greedy sort, soldiers who had used their uniforms to excuse their violence, religious figures, both good and shifty, who had walked great distances to be present. But to this wilderness dweller, they were all the same. The river might not be polluted, he told them with bold, blunt words, but they certainly were. "Snakes" he called some of them, yet they listened soberly.

Then came his most daring words. "Go down into this river with me," he commanded, "and let me dip you under as a sign to your fellows that you're sorry for your wrongs." They obeyed. Gripped by a power they couldn't explain, they went down and came out drenched, determined to live more honest lives.

Into this charged atmosphere came one man who was different. He had never played at religion. By His own astounding claim, He had never sinned. He was a Good Man, really good, through and through.

Yet He approached the fiery orator and said, "Take me down into the river, too." There was protest, but the Good Man prevailed. They went down together and He, too, came out of the waters, drenched.

Then it happened. The Good Man stood for a few moments, eyes raised to the skies above, as though in rapt meditation. He saw a dovelike bird come out of those skies. And out of those skies He heard a voice saying, "You are my Son, my unique Son; I'm very pleased with you." For Him it became an unforgettable moment.

This Good Man gained a following, and when He died His followers were shattered. They felt as though in knowing Him they had known God himself. Then, on the third day after His death they found His grave empty. Empty! And in the weeks to follow He kept appearing to them, eating with them, telling them what to do, like a leader. Little by little, doubts melted and an astounding conviction took hold of them: He is alive!

A few days later, this Living One was taken out of their sight. Immediately they began to preserve incidents from His amazing life, and this incident by the river was one of them. There He had taken His place with sinners. Someone even remembered an ancient preacher's words. He had forseen that God would send a Unique One who would be "numbered with the transgressors." They were sure this was He.

From then till the present, this Living One has attracted followers. Nearly always they acknowledge the beginning of His leadership over them with a ceremony using water. Sometimes they are immersed in it. Sometimes it is poured over them. The ceremony is conducted in crocodile-infested rivers, in well-appointed buildings, even in hospitals. Nearly anywhere.

Why? It is a matter of identification. If He could go down into the river to identify with sinners, they say, they can use water to identify with Him. It is a matter of obedience. He commanded it. It is a symbolic way of saying the old has ended, new life has begun. It is a way of bearing witness to an inner cleansing. It is a joy.

The fiery orator was John the Baptist, the river, Jordan. The Living One is Jesus, the Christ. He is Lord of all!

Chapter 23

Divorce and the Spirit of Jesus

In the *D* section of a fourteen-hundred-page biblical reference book, the word *divorce* is listed as follows, "Divorce — See Marriage."

It's as though one should turn in a medical reference work to the word *disease* and find, "Disease — See Health."

Divorce is related to the failure of marriage somewhat as disease is related to the failure of health.

Therefore, to think as a Christian on the subject of divorce, one must first think as a Christian on the subject of marriage. He must think as Jesus thought.

The Pharisees tried to trap Jesus on the subject. Moses' law had made provision for divorce (Deuteronomy 24:1). How, they wanted to know, was the provision to be interpreted?

In response to them Jesus admitted the reality of divorce as a social fact of life. But He pointed the Pharisees back beyond the time of Moses to the original nature of things.

In Matthew's account of this exchange (19:3-12)

at least three truths about the interior nature of marriage stand out.

Marriage, in the first place, is a divine institution. It is more than merely a relationship which a man and woman establish. It is an estate they enter.

Moses' divorce provision was indeed a concession to human sinfulness. It was ordered, however, to blunt the damage done by unregulated marital breakups, requiring that the breakups at least be formalized by legal writs.

Jesus admitted this. But He went on to say, "From the beginning it was not so" (Matthew 19:8), pointing to God's intention.

Not all interpreters agree with the Lutheran idea that marriage is an "order of creation" implied in the origin of man. But a reverent reading of Matthew and Genesis makes it difficult to say less about the profundity of the relationship.

Marriage, in the second place, is an exclusive relationship between one man and one woman. Monogamy, we call it.

"For this reason," Jesus said, quoting further from the story of Adam and Eve, "a man shall leave his father and mother and be joined to his wife, and the two shall become one" (Matthew 19:5, RSV).

Multiple marriages — bigamy, polygamy, serial divorces — abounded in Bible times as they abound in ours. The Bible nowhere explicitly forbids them, but wherever they appear their evil effects — insecurity, jealousy, favoritism — are evident.

Over against these facts, we place Jesus' words. Monogamy is God's intention, He says, and this becomes a principle to follow.

Marriage, in the third place, is a "one flesh" relationship. To the secular Western mind, the expression stands for physical union. To the Hebrew mind, it stood for the total merging of two personalities — their hopes, fears, strengths, and weaknesses — and this spiritual fact was sacramentalized in physical union.

Hence, marriage is more than the association of things. It is the becoming *one* thing. Although neither party surrenders his individuality, the two lives are merged in a higher reality to which their individuality is subordinated. All this is implied in "one flesh."

Such lofty views of marriage raise for us the same question they raised for Jesus' contemporaries. Is there any ground on which a marriage may be dissolved?

In considering the question one thinks of the great numbers — neighbors, relatives, confidants — who know divorce not only as a legal concept but also as a brutal fact. They know the loneliness, vulnerability, and guilt it introduces. They know grimly the numerous threads of the social fabric it slashes and leaves dangling.

But thinking of these hurt persons only reinforces the importance of Jesus' serious view of marriage. It reinforces too the validity of allowing only one ground for divorce — adultery.

The reason that adultery is made the one exception to the inviolability of marriage is that it, of itself, disrupts the ''one flesh'' relationship by bringing into it a third party. If divorce were not permitted on this ground, a tacit sanction of polygamy would result.

In the spirit of the gospel, however, even adultery might better be dealt with — whenever possible — by forgiveness and reconciliation rather than by divorce. The cost of forgiveness is enormous, as those who have paid it know, but the cost of divorce is still greater.

In the face of today's casualness about divorce, Christians are called upon to hold a high view of the marriage relationship for one major reason: Jesus did.

But following His example takes some doing. Does a high view call for a legalistic rigor in which law matters but persons do not count? Does it call for a sentimentality in which persons count but law does not matter?

Jesus respected the laws regulating marriage, and He loved compassionately the persons whose marriages had failed. We will never do both as well as He did, but it is our obligation to try.

All the while, we Christians are called upon to demonstrate in flesh and blood that Christian marriage is a glad-hearted commitment of one man and one woman each to the other and both to God.

Committed love, Christ's kind of sacrificial caring, makes the bond of marriage so healthy that divorce doesn't have a chance.

Chapter 24

Divorce Does More Damage than You Think

At first the conversation was calm. Then the signals of anger began to crackle between them. In minutes, Dan and Carol were threatening each other with divorce. What made the situation unusual was that the three of us had met to talk over their approaching wedding.

These two young people were demonstrating an attitude widely held in the western world: divorce is a casual matter. But I'm convinced, after twenty-one years as a pastor in three widely seperated North American cities, that divorce is as devasting an experience as it ever was. Every time one is granted — an average of nearly three thousand times a day on this continent — shock waves go in all directions.

Take the case of a couple divorced one month. He used to fume when she "yakked" on the phone. Now he can't stand the silence. When he slumped in front of the TV all Saturday afternoon she used to boil. Now her set runs when there's no one in front of it. Neither expected this.

One man said the hardest thing for him after his divorce was to stop saying "we." All divorced persons feel this to a degree. They sense that some deep unity has been severed.

Or take the case of a divorce that has been final for twenty years. The nightmare should be long forgotten. Now the baby of the dissolved marriage, twenty-three years old, announces she will have a church wedding. Mother will sit on the left front pew, of course. Will father attend? If he does, should he sit next or behind? Should father or stepfather be in the reception line?

A young woman's big day is clouded or spoiled. She comes to the altar frightened and near tears. I've seen it happen. Our traditions still assume that marital stability is the norm. Every divorce counters this, tearing the social fabric a little more.

The children of a divorce are thrust into their own maze of unforeseen problems. What if they feel Dad has deserted them and they don't want to see him but he has visiting privileges? Or if they want to be loyal to both parents but they can't because Mother and Dad fight each other through them?

Children experience enough stresses outside the home. When a divorce shatters the home itself, they feel defenseless. They suffer in silence but not without consequences.

I remember a depressed twenty-year-old girl. At twelve, she had been the silent observer to her parents' divorce. Now, for eight years she had felt that she had contributed to the breakup, not an uncommon feeling for children. When I met her, she was blaming herself for almost everything that went wrong in life.

Divorced persons often feel angry or abandoned — sometimes for years. They can't resolve these feelings because the person they involve is alive but no longer around. They become so emotionally wretched they don't want to live. The suicide rate is higher for divorced persons.

In our culture, marriage is still one of life's most important enterprises. Because of this, the divorced live with unspoken feelings of failure. One woman was asking herself twenty-seven years years after the divorce, "What did I do wrong?"

Then there's guilt. What does God say about what I've done? It's not so commonly asked now as a generation ago, but it is asked more often than you think. Ministers hear it.

Divorced persons themselves feel like displaced persons. They are no longer at ease with their former single friends because they're no longer single. They get the cool treatment from their married friends; they're no longer married. This adds loneliness to the lingering aftereffects — a loneliness they scarcely need. Alcohol is only one of the refuges they seek.

One of the most unexpected aftereffects of a divorce is moral vulnerability. Divorced persons feel they have failed; they feel angry; they need to know they are desirable. In this state of mind they are far from morally stable. Moreover, exploiters abound in every community. Did Jesus mean this when He said, ''He who divorces his wife causes her to commit adultery''?

A divorce is sometimes necessary, and some persons are divorced against their wishes (abandoned like an old car). A divorce may be the lesser of two evils; and sometimes out of one, good emerges. Even so, divorce is a wrenching experience — too wrenching to justify our current casualness.

Take, for example, the case of Dan and Carol. Would they have stung each other so blithely with threats of divorce even before they were married if they had known the facts? Fortunately they were open to help and are now happily married.

Thousands of troubled spouses need to know also that there are options to divorce. Three weeks ago I got a letter from a couple whose marriage at one time looked impossible. They used to scream abuse at each other over the heads of three cowering children. Periodically they walked out, and one separation lasted several months.

But somehow they couldn't give up on a covenant they had made. They kept in touch, repeatedly asking for help and doggedly trying. Even after things began to mend, there were slips and restarts.

Their recent letter brought me up to date. There's a humility in their attitudes toward each other now. Without losing sight of their strengths, they're more realistic about their own weaknesses. They've found it easier to see and compliment the good things in each other since they've learned to pray together. They're growing up; their love is growing up too.

Don't think they haven't paid a price. At times it has seemed exorbitant. But taking everything into account, it has cost far less than a divorce.

Chapter 25

Striving Ministers

One minister spent half his time angry at his congregation. He was a striver, and whenever his people did not see things his way, his prospects for success were jeopardized and his anger ignited.

We could conclude that anyone called to a special ministry for the Lord should not strive. But that would be contrary to human nature. We might better conclude that Christian workers should be sure to strive in the right way.

The Apostle Paul was a striver. He wrote to the Colossians, "I want you to know how greatly I strive for you, and for those at Laodicea, and for all who have not seen my face" (2:1, RSV).

It's no timid word, this word *to strive*. It suggests "a passionate struggle, a constantly renewed concentration of forces on the attainment of a goal." Striving in Paul's day was what athletes did, and from the Greek word we get our English word *to agonize*.

All who want to strive for the Lord in a right way will find Paul's testimony instructive. From Colossians 1:24 — 2:5, here are some of his leading ideas.

The Apostle tells us, for one thing, that his strivings were in accord with a prescribed message. "I became a minister" of the body of Christ, he says, "to make the word of God fully known" (1:25, RSV).

This Word of God, the Old Testament as fulfilled and interpreted in Jesus Christ, was no leaden word, however; no word to be merely stored safely in synagogues. Proclaimed, it was a Word with power to give men life.

His subjection to it arrests us when we recall that his own words were by no means limited. They came out of an inventive mind, well stored with ideas and conversant with the thought forms of his age.

Nevertheless, the Word of God to him was a "given" to faith. However inventively he clothed it, making it current to his times, the Word itself was irrevocable. Having it, he needed to strive, not for novelty, but only for ways to make it fully known.

The Apostle tells us, for another thing, that his strivings always kept the individual in view. He proclaimed Christ, "warning every man and teaching every man in all wisdom, that [he might] present every man mature in Christ" (1:28, RSV).

Whether or not these words are a reply to false teachings, they show the Apostle's awareness of the one-by-one dimension of Christian work. He never lost the individual in the throng.

We are inclined to. Mass-oriented as our world has become, it may trick us into seeing work for Christ only in terms of throngs. On the contrary, the task of bringing men to maturity in Him is often a one-by-one ministry — the quiet guidance of a high school lad, the restoration to faith of someone who has lost his way.

Striving which does not keep this in mind may be energetic but unfocused.

The Apostle tells us, for a third thing, that his strivings were in behalf of Christ's body in the world. Exertion for the sake of the individual is, for the Christian worker, only one dimension of the task. Concern for the corporate life of the church is the other.

So constant is this concern to the Apostle, in fact, that in the present passage there is direct or indirect reference to the church in every verse.

All Paul's strivings on behalf of individuals were, consequently, "that their hearts may be encouraged as they are knit together in love" (2:2, RSV). He wanted every believer's life to be enhanced by his organic participation in the life of Christ's church.

What large aspirations all this holds before us — to make the Word of God fully known, to warn and instruct every man, to promote the unity of Christ's church in the world.

In times like ours, however, even this kind of talk has a way of prompting anger. Laymen may be cued by it to see more clearly the deficiencies of ministers — real or imagined. Paid Christian workers may be sensitized to the disloyalties of laymen — real or imagined.

Paul's words can serve a better purpose than that. They can give us a standard by which to measure the intensity of our own exertions for Christ's cause. In a world which seems less than one lap from fiery judgment, we should all be striving ministers.

Chapter 26

How Warm Is the Spirit?

This morning, a thousand miles from home, I went to church. Leaving my motel at 9:15, I drove across a corner of this Colorado city in brilliant sunshine and within ten minutes parked my car at a church I had never seen before.

The community surrounding the church was obviously upper middle class: large ranch-style houses surrounded by well-coiffed shrubs and well-kept lawns, streets curving gracefully to meet at odd angles.

The church fit the setting: a steep-roofed sanctuary, a smaller, steep-roofed chapel, joined by a one-story Christian education facility. It was a simple and inviting structure, the obvious result of intelligent planning.

I walked the long sidewalk fronting the building and, slightly self-conscious, entered the large foyer. Three dignified-looking men were there talking to one another. I hesitated. Were they ushers? None spoke, so I crossed the foyer and stepped into the large, open, blue-carpeted area at the back of the nave. One usher stood at the back of each of the three aisles.

I moved uncertainly toward the center aisle and again hesitated. The usher on the aisle, a man of forty or fifty whose gray suit highlighted the gray in his long sideburns, handed me two papers but did not speak. Ill at ease, I moved past him toward an aisle seat about a third of the way forward.

The sanctuary was awe-inspiring. A royal-blue carpet filled the center aisle, mounted the chancel steps, and splayed out to surround the lectern, Communion table, and pulpit — like a quiet lake. From the chancel floor a blue-velvet reredos rose to the peak, backing a walnut cross. The architecture and decor could not be faulted.

The bookrack in front of me held no hymnal. It was an oversight easy to understand, but what was I to do? I did not feel like a visitor, usually a pleasant enough experience; rather, I felt like a stranger and much too restrained to help myself. When it came time to sing the hymns, I solved the problem by standing where I could look between the heads of the man and the woman in front of me. Relying more on memory and imagination than on vision, I sang most of the words.

After the announcements, ushers passed little books and pencils down the pews, and each worshiper was carefully instructed to sign his name and list his address. I signed, but I wondered how warm I would feel two weeks hence when I would get a card back home saying how nice it was to have me in church.

The minister's sermon was about Paul's call to Macedonia, the call to meet human need. There were opportunities, he said, in the Peace Corps, VISTA, politics, even in the home. It was a well-ordered sermon, and at its close we sang two stanzas of "Jesus Calls Us."

When the benediction ended, I took my cue from those around me and stepped quickly into the aisle. My eyes met those of a man moving out of the back pew. When our eyes met the second time, we nodded slightly at each other. By the time I reached the open area, I was behind three women, fiftyish or so, who were talking vigorously. One volunteered to the others that her husband was out on the lake with his brother, fishing. They all laughed. It was only minutes since we had heard of Paul's crossing the Aegean on an urgent Christian mission.

The minister was in the foyer where the three dignified men had been. He was talking warmly to some man at the head of the line. I joined the line, waited awkwardly a few moments. Then, following the lead of others, I stepped outside and walked to my car. In sixty minutes among "fellow believers," not one voice had addressed me, not one hand engaged mine.

Everything had been nice. The organ music was well chosen and played, the bulletin flawless, and the sermon carefully prepared. But, I thought as I drove down the gently curving streets, what if I had gone to the church desperate for an alternative to suicide? What if I had been seeking courage to avoid selling my soul in a shady business deal? Or, what if I had been wanting help to give a wobbly marriage one final try? I think I might have left disillusioned or perhaps downright angry.

I am aware that I could have glad-handed my way into the foyer. I could have waited boldly at the close and with a flourish made myself known to the minister. But I was much too self-conscious. When you are an outsider in a strange church, you need the help of the insiders.

I know also that you go to church to worship God, but that's not the whole of it. You go to worship God in fellowship of warmhearted believers. That's why I went to church instead of picking up a televised service in my motel room.

I am sure the people I sat among today are typical human beings, each with his heartaches, his secrets, his spiritual longings. Why then was this not reflected?

Here's a guess: These people are members not only of the church but of the American cult of success as well. Many modern churchmen are. In this cult, frailties and failings are kept out of sight. People must appear completely adequate for life at any cost. The result is an antiseptic niceness that denies any sense of sin or need of grace.

I don't mean to seem harsh. I am a churchman and have often pleaded for the church against its critics. Now I catch myself asking, "Is this part of the 'Establishment' the young inveigh against? Is this a society of nice people who deny their own needs and so are incapable of feeling compassion for the needs of others?"

My thoughts turn also to my own congregation

back home in Illinois. Our sanctuary is lovely — just renovated, in fact — and our people are fine, generous to a fault. When I return, they will welcome me warmly. I am one of them.

But after this morning I am asking how they would treat a visitor from Colorado. Has the Holy Spirit made them capable of the kind of loving concern an outsider requires? Has He given them that supernatural warmth that unites them in loving fellowship and at the same time keeps them open to the lonely and needy who come among them?

One hour in another church has given me a fresh and uneasy perspective. I keep saying, "So that's the way it feels to go to church when you don't belong." Does it feel that way in the congregation I'm a part of?

It is no idle question, and I need to know the answer. I am the pastor.

Reprinted from *Together* magazine, July, 1972.
Copyright © 1972 by the United Methodist Publishing House.

Chapter 27

Who Cares?

Ron and Milton were at it again. Their wives, Ginny and Ruth, bustled about the kitchen, putting the final garnishes on a Sunday dinner.

In a bedroom directly above them their four girls laughed and argued their way through a game of Chinese checkers. The fifth, Denise, Ron's hungry two-and-a-half-year-old, wailed intermittently and otherwise kept the game in an uproar.

The noise tumbled down the stairwell in bursts and spilled into the living room where Ron and Milton sat. But they didn't hear it. They had their own skirmish mounted — a usual Sunday afternoon occurrence.

"If the children of a hard-drinking father need food," Ron argued, "the church ought to dip into the offering plate to help them even if they've never been around the place. God is on the side of the needy, isn't He? Then why not give them God's funds?"

"Yes," Milton countered, "but those offerings were given for special causes — like evangelism and missions. You can't just grab them for any need. You have to respect the givers' wishes. Why not a special offering for special needs?''

Their subject was always religion. They were both committed churchmen. Today, the debate was over religion and money.

Debates like this were never resolved. Ron always came out on one side, Milt on the other. They loved to argue, but it was more than that. Somehow, they had different starting points when they talked about religion.

"You're an old liberal," Milt said, wryly.

"You're a dyed-in-the-wool conservative from back in the hills," Ron shot back, breaking into a baritone laugh. They lapsed into silence.

Milt stood up, stretched his arms toward the ceiling, and then bent to poke the fire. Ron got up and walked, hands behind his back, to the window overlooking the street.

It was a blustery fall day. Rain and a high wind the night before had carpeted the street with soggy yellow leaves.

Along this drenched thoroughfare an ancient black Ford glided into view, slipping ever so slightly on the leaves. Ron knew the car from the dented right fender. It was Mrs. Thornton's. She was at the wheel.

Milton joined Ron at the window just as the car slowed for the stop sign at the corner. They watched the brake lights go out, and the car swung cautiously southward. Neither spoke.

They had both seen Mrs. Thornton in church only an hour before. They knew she hadn't had time to eat her solitary noon meal. Each man guessed in silence her reason for being out. Laura Thornton's life was known.

In the trunk of her car, Milt thought, she's probably got a cardboard box and inside that a pressure cooker and inside that two quarts or so of steaming stew.

Ron had similar thoughts, but his mind jumped ahead. Where is Laura Thornton off to this time?

With a flash he rembered that only the past Wednesday the siren had called volunteer firemen to the south edge of town. A family of four had been burned out. The father, a heavy drinker, was out of work too.

The state welfare office had moved them to a rundown trailer park where the rent was cheap. Laura Thornton, Ron thought, is likely on her way there with her stew — or whatever she has in her box.

Ron broke the silence. "She's quite a gal, isn't she?" He remembered the uncomfortably hot August afternoon he had moved his family to town. The same black Ford, much shinier then and minus the dent, had brought Laura to their door with a fresh-baked pie. It had brightened his wife's spirits that day.

Milton had his own reflections. When his neighbor died of emphysema, Laura Thornton was there to help.

Come to think of it, two years later when Milt's first girl was born, it was Laura who brought a gift to the door and uttered a faltering invitation for them to attend church. He and Ruth hadn't responded right away, but the invitation stuck.

Ron and Milton dropped back into their chairs.

"Where were we now?" Ron asked with a

gentle chuckle. Milt couldn't remember.

Neither was able to get the discussion going again.

Then, Ginny rang the little brass dinner bell on the dining room table. An upstairs bedroom door was wrenched open, and children pounded down the stairs. Denise followed, clutching the spindles of the handrail firmly, letting herself down a step at a time, and wailing, "Wait for me."

At the table, the children were a little hard to tame. They attacked the food with zest, arguing, when they could not be shushed, about the unfinished game on the table upstairs.

Some sort of quietness hung over Ron and Milton as they worked white meat free from chicken breasts. Even pumpkin pie at the end didn't dispel it.

Chapter 28

Give Your Pastor a Break, Not a Breakdown

There are three kinds of pastors.

There are men whose work for the Lord flourishes wherever they go. The rest of us look at them with awe and a little envy (of a good sort, I hope).

There are men who fail. We all put ourselves into this class at times, but it is really made up of men either untrained for the task, inept in its finer skills, short on integrity, or lacking in commitment.

The majority of pastors are neither. They are committed men, but sometimes their grand visions have faded under the glaring realities of their work — thankless labors, economic stresses, and a lack of hearty support from the laymen they try to lead.

If you are a layman, you can help your pastor succeed — without patronizing him. You may, in fact, have the power to give him a break or a breakdown. Here are some questions to ponder.

1. Do I put myself in my pastor's shoes before making harsh judgments?

Your pastor works from an unrelenting sense

that God has called him. Even if his motives are less worthy, there must be some good reasons he is working where he is. Try to find them.

Remember, however, that his noblest aspirations are filtered into life through a flawed humanity. Your pastor's mental powers may not come up to your standards. His social graces may need polishing. He may not seem as "spiritual" as you think he could be.

If so, deal with these deficiencies, even if they are unacceptable, by giving him the same right to be less than perfect that you grant yourself. Then, try to appreciate your pastor's situation, living as he does in the last third of the twentieth century.

He is supposed to speak for eternal realities, but he lives in a world strongly committed to the here and now. He sometimes feels out of step, and should, but if he has the sensitivities his calling requires, he cannot be out of step without being aware of it.

Moreover, he gets little reinforcement of his worth as a minister from a here-and-now culture. Sometimes, in fact, his worth is subtly devalued by secular influences within the church. He is not God's man if he quits for such reasons, but you can help him to become more fully God's man if you try to put yourself in his shoes before judging him harshly.

2. Have I found ways to let my pastor know I appreciate him?

If you're going to do it by words, make them pointed. For example, "Thanks for calling on Mother; she rested after you left." Or, "Our fifteen-year-old got your idea about honesty without hostility." These are better than the thanks-for-everything type of commendation.

Your pastor always works in areas where progress is hard to measure. An alcoholic friend at the newspaper office I used to visit seemed to understand this. "Hi, Reverend," he would call across the room for everyone to hear when I entered. "How's everything in the world of the intangibles?"

What keeps him going, then? A perpetually renewed sense that God has called him, an occasional flash in the eye of a new Christian, a warm word now and then from a grateful parishioner — these are the sorts of things.

3. If I am in serious disagreement with my pastor, do I talk to him directly?

Some parishioners tell their prayer circle or confide their disagreement to a few people by telephone. Others lock it up inside to fester. There are more righteous ways to handle a disagreement. Go to your pastor quietly and with as much grace as possible try to talk it out.

You may hesitate to do so, fearing your pastor will not keep your confidence — one of the most unforgivable breaches of his ethics. Even so, weigh the peril of such a breach against the possibility of a resolved conflict.

Whenever you speak directly to your pastor about a point of serious disagreement, you run the risk of discovering in the process his own private griefs. They are there, though they are dealt with in faith. Pastors too are vulnerable to disappointment, discouragement, and even depression. Glimpse this and you may temper your disagreement with forgiveness.

4. Do my dissatisfactions with my pastor reflect my own spiritual deficiency?

Some people are down on their pastors as an alternative to being down on their sins.

Consider this checklist: Am I bothered by unconfessed sins? If so, my pastor may be my whipping boy. Do I feel a little too good for the church — a cut above ordinary Christians? This spirit always creates friction. Do I have hidden strivings to "take over" so that my pastor is really my competitor? Such hidden problems are often involved in a break with a pastor.

5. Do I pray with conviction for my pastor?

Frank Laubach, in his book, *Prayer: The Mightiest Force in the World,* says the very quality of a pastor's voice brightens when someone prays for him while he is speaking. The opposite happens when he is bombarded by negative attitudes.

Your prayers can gently take down barriers, shrink disagreements, or at the least, make charity possible where accord is not. Prayer, moreover, can set in motion reconciling providences.

To sum up, you have more to do with your pastor's successes than you realize. It has often been said that great churches make great pastors.

What your pastor may need is to see in your countenance and feel in your handshake that you are for him, and to sense that together you are for Christ. Signal him this message regularly, and you will give him a break — and, perhaps, your church a breakthrough.

Chapter 29

The Laying On of Hands

Four hundred people sat reverently in our dimly lit sanctuary. The altar, more brightly lighted, was solidly lined with petitioners.

Donald Demaray, our special speaker, P. G. Hampton, a machinist from our congregation, and I moved slowly down the line. We listened to whispered expressions of need, laid hands on bowed heads and prayed, anointing with oil.

I suddenly realized what a personal thing we were doing. You just don't go around laying your hands on other people's heads. Most people feel very sensitive about this part of their bodies.

As we moved, I remembered also what a warm and loving fellowship the first generation of believers had. They laid hands on new converts for the receiving of the Holy Spirit. (Remember Ananias's coming to Saul at Damascus?) They laid hands on the sick, too.

Did they learn the laying on of hands from Jesus? At least, did the practice get reinforcement from Him? He used His hands often to show focused concern.

When Simon's mother-in-law was sick in bed

with fever, for example, He took her by the hand and helped her up.

He took a blind man by the hand, leading him aside from the crowd. (What a considerate man He was!) He touched him and then a second time touched his eyes, restoring his sight fully.

He touched lepers, lame men. He laid His hands on children. You find quite a few such references in the New Testament when you start looking.

No wonder His followers in all ages, when in the flush of devotion to Him, have shown love and compassion by the laying on of hands.

But it is no superficial thing they do. We have just come through a period when all sorts of liberties have been taken with the bodies of others. Sometimes, it has been done in the guise of sensitivity training — of a bizarre kind — and sometimes even in the name of love.

The result of this sort of laying on of hands has often been disillusionment and a trail of guilty memories.

The church at its best has too much respect for the worth of persons to trifle with their bodies so. It even reflects this respect in some of its instructions for ordination.

Paul wrote to Timothy, for example, "Lay hands suddenly on no man." He meant, "Don't ordain novices to the highly personal ministry of serving the family of God."

If a person is to have access to a sick room or to share in the secrets of a failing marriage, he had better be more than a young Christian, however enthusiastic. He had better be a person of tried character and loving restraint.

Is it this concern that love be under holy discipline that leads Bible writers sometimes to link hand and heart together? "Cleanse your hands, you sinners," wrote James, "and purify your hearts, you men of double mind" (4:8, RSV). Psalm 24 makes the same connection.

In the Christian church, hearts and hands must be under the same holy control. Integrity demands it, because what's in the heart, for good or ill, will come out in the hands.

The need for the laying on of hands is great these days. People of all ages feel alienated from God, from one another, and often even from themselves. Loving hands, under the guidance of Jesus Christ, can become great ministers for good.

Why not, then, begin to pray for a renewal of the ministry of the laying on of hands? Here are some suggestions.

Let us pray God's Spirit to raise up in every church seasoned officers who know how to minister with their hands — responsibly, compassionately, and in life-giving ways.

Let us relearn the ministry of laying hands on the elderly, not only at the altar but in the church aisle, in their homes, and wherever loneliness isolates them.

Let us teach our young greater respect for the God-given dignity of others. We can show them by example and spell it out in clear Anglo-Saxon words. There is no more effective way to wean them from the irresponsible handling of others, so common these days — and often so damaging.

Let us revive the practice of prayer and the laying on of hands for the sick. This should not be done as a manner of "stunt" healing. Nor should it be accompanied by rash promises in the name of God. We are all mortal and must live and die as mortals. Early Christians who saw that not all believers are healed in this life learned to talk of "the healing of immortality."

If we can be biblical, the laying on of hands can become a marvelous way of focusing love and sharing the burdens of other believers. And, through the laying on of hands, our sovereign Lord may see fit at times to grant miraculous healings.

Chapter 30

"I'm Thinking About Death"

Leonard Drake, fifty-two, lay alone in room 18, mercifully strapped to a Stryker frame. His ashen face was gaunt and bony.

I sat down near his head, exchanged a few words, then asked, "What are you thinking about these days, Len?"

With effort, but calmly, he said, "I'm thinking about death." There was no trace of fear in his voice, no sign that he was responding as a trapped and angry man. His half-whispered words were matter-of-fact and seemed strangely fortified with hope.

More than a year earlier, Len's doctor, a Christian, had broken the news to him. Some bone cancer has no known cure. At the time, he had suggested he talk to a minister.

Ministers were not Len's kind of people. In his fifty-two years he had seen inside a church no more than a dozen times. He didn't follow the suggestion.

Nine months later, his name appeared on the hospital list, and I called on him. Few preliminaries were necessary. He listened readily to words about Jesus' love for sinners and His death for their salvation. Like a child he confessed his sins and received Jesus into his life. The doctor's concern had apparently not been wasted.

The next day I found Len poring over an old Bible he had got somewhere, and, always after that, our talks centered on Jesus. Len was reading avidly about Him.

Nevertheless, during the three months following his conversion, Len went through the usual stages of coming to terms with death.

Sometimes he doubted he was really going to die. He didn't say so, but one could sense it. Occasionally there was strong emotion — frustration, maybe — as though he would fight death off by sheer grit. Once or twice there were hints that he wanted to bargain with God — "Spare my life and I'll. . . ."

Gradually he came to be at peace. It was a confident peace, not mere resignation or drugged tranquillity. It was a state of mind in which he was able to experience God as mightier than all the destructive forces of life. He was at this stage the day he said, "I'm thinking about death."

He lingered only a few weeks longer; his strength ebbed, his discomfort grew, but as long as he could communicate, Jesus was real and His promises adequate. I saw in Leonard Drake the reality of Christian hope in the face of death.

I saw that the Christian faith, taken seriously, gives the process of dying a new aspect. Len was never cavalier about it. Death hunched on his pathway; dying was to be his final ordeal, and he prayed often for courage.

Yet, as he pored over his New Testament at first, and later listened supinely to its assurances, he saw in Jesus one who was mightier than death.

Through Him, death had lost its sting (I Corinthians 15:55). In Jesus he had gained present resurrection power (John 11:25). By identification with Him, in one sense he had already died and been resurrected to eternal life (Colossians 3:1-4).

I saw also that this hope does not spare a Christian from the ordeal of dying, with all it entails. For Leonard there were moments of denial. There were impulses to bargain. There were periods of momentary anger and resentment.

How else could it be for a creature to whom death is so contrary to all he believes about his destiny? How else could it be when God had invested him with such a powerful impulse to survive?

Len met these turbulent moments of the spirit in faith. I could not give him false hopes of getting well. But he sensed an unconditional confidence in God, coming from someone near him, whom he loved and trusted.

As I reflect on the ordeal now from a distance, I see that the biblical hope could save many Leonards from going down blind alleys when their own encounter with death comes slowly and with long forewarning.

There is a time to talk about divine healing. Both in the Bible and out we have records of salvation from death in response to faith. But to the dying, divine healing must be talked about sensitively, in a mood of reverent inquiry and in the confidence that God's goodness is not canceled by physical death.

If God is sovereign over His creatures, all options must be left open to Him. Isn't death one option?

When I think of Len's dying, one question lingers longest with me. He was fifty-two years old, biblically illiterate and wasting with disease. But he came alive to God and in three months absorbed the deep assurances of the Scriptures about the believer's hope of life forever with Jesus.

Who can measure what the unrealized possibilities are for believers who have had health and many years to mature the Christian hope?

Chapter 31

No Helicopter Lifts to the Mountains of God

You're on high ground in mountain country. You have little protection from sudden squalls. Nights get cold and wild animals lurk.

Your guide points across a wide valley to a distant range, majestic against the sky. "There," he tells you, "the sun always shines. There you don't breathe pollution, mountain gales don't buffet, and wild beasts are unknown.

"Best of all," he says, still pointing at the lofty range, "one dwells there who is glorious beyond words. He receives into fellowship those who come to him."

You respond, "I want to go."

Your guide beckons, but not upward. You start down into the valley. The path becomes treacherous. At times, it threads through chilly canyons. Wild beasts seem near.

Every time you feel almost ready to turn back, the path opens into a wide place. The distant range is nearer and awesomely grand. You are reminded of the Presence. You say, "Let's go on," and the journey continues.

It's fiction, of course. But it pictures two of

many things about the Christian life reflected in Romans 5:1-5. According to this passage the Christian life has in it intertwining elements of hope and hardships.

Hope is the expectation that someday we shall see God in His glory. We shall be with Him. We are with Him now, of course, but we are limited by our circumstances. "The time will come," Paul says "when we shall see reality whole and face to face!" (I Corinthians 13:12, Phillips).

Who can imagine the glory of God? When Moses returned from Sinai, his face shone. He had been in God's presence and his face reflected the glory. The tabernacle in the wilderness was marked by the Shekinah of God's presence. The disciples discerned the same splendor in Jesus. "We beheld his glory," John wrote.

Yet as marvelous as these historic revelations were, they were only partial and preliminary. The unspeakable splendor of God is yet to be fully unveiled. We look forward to it with hope as we move toward the mountains of God.

Hope, then, keeps us going. It is our confidence in a glorious future. It is our expectation of splendor beyond words. It is renewed by our recurrent glances toward the horizon.

But alongside it, we lay Paul's other word, *hardships.* (A valley must be crossed, and there are no helicopter lifts to the mountains of God.) Hardships are a part of every Christian journey.

Tribulations, the King James Version translates the word. *Trials and troubles,* Phillips paraphrases it. *Sufferings,* we read in the Revised Standard Version. Whichever of these alternatives we choose, none speaks of an experience we want, but each reflects an aspect of life known to every believer. Hardships meet us all in the valley of our mortality.

Yet, the hope on our horizon makes the winds and squalls of this life worthwhile. Note Paul's progression of thought. Hardships "produce endurance." They develop constancy in holding out under trial. "Endurance produces character." It builds into life the quality of sturdiness. And "character produces [more] hope."

To the new believer, hope may be little more than a doctrine to be believed. But the successful meeting of adversity nourishes it into a sustaining conviction. And, in the valleys, the fresh glimpses of the mountains of God and the anticipation of His glory raise it to a sense of eager certainty.

If the Christian life is really an intertwining of hope and hardships, shall we then resolve to bear this world's sufferings with resignation because things will be better in another world? Paul has something loftier in mind. Resignation is only one aspect of the Christian mentality. The other aspect is rejoicing.

"We rejoice in our hope," Paul says. The mountains are there, and the Presence awaits us. We rejoice in hardships too, he adds. We are in the valley, the perils stalk us, but God is bigger than the perils; and the mountains are beyond. Even a chilly canyon can become a place for joy.

It was this kind of all-encompassing certainty that made Annie Johnson Flint write:

The danger that His love allows
   Is safer than our fears may know;
The peril that His care permits
   Is our defense where'er we go.

Chapter 32

Something Remarkable Is Going On!

The twenty-seven-year-old man who just left my room reminds me again that across this great continent, something remarkable is going on.

It isn't that the crime rate is dropping. (It's not.)

It isn't that drug abuse is declining. (Reports say it's on the rise.)

In spite of these bleak facts, what's happening, though not as visible as crime and drug abuse, is nevertheless remarkable: a whole generation is beginning to talk and act as if there were a supernatural dimension to life.

Some people, without knowing what they're doing, grudgingly acknowledge the supernatural — in a negative way. A man may point to an estate he's pulled together for a family coming apart and lament, "There's got to be more to life than this."

Some people talk about a supernatural realm in a dangerous way. "Perhaps there's something to all this stuff about witches and mediums and horoscopes and Satan worship," they say.

The occult is, after all, one way of believing in the supernatural. Dangerous or not, in America alone more than two hundred fifty thousand people are said to be actively practicing witchcraft.

But growing numbers of people, like the twenty-seven-year-old man I have mentioned, say simply — "God."

What they mean by "God" is breathtaking to think of. They mean the God who gave the whole world existence and who personally is in touch with it every moment, keeping it going. They mean the God of the Bible, the God and father of our Lord Jesus Christ. These people say He has made himself known to them.

Only yesterday, at a friend's garage out south of town, I met a man who has recently come alive to God and the unseen world. Bearded and in shabby jeans, he was silently studying the greasy engine of a red Willys Jeep when he began to talk.

"You've heard of these Jesus People?" he asked. Then scarcely stopping to acknowledge my nod he said, "Well, I'm one of them."

"I didn't used to believe in God or Jesus or heaven or nothin'," he volunteered. In his own colloquial way, he filled this statement out, saying, in effect that he once was a naturalist but when he got converted to Christ he became a supernaturalist.

One man's testimony alone, however, may not be enough for you. What, in a Christian sense, is a supernaturalist?

The answer goes in this direction: Life has more to it than our senses can experience. It's bigger than we can squeeze into a lifetime. Its yearnings are deeper than booze or beauty or bounty can satisfy. It has an unseen dimension, which is as real and important as the dimension we can see and touch.

Or, to come at it as the Bible does, life begins with God, life continues with God, and life with God never ends. For from Him and through Him and to Him are all things. To Him be glory forever. Amen.

This newfound conviction gave a bearded member of the Jesus People reason to live. It delivered a twenty-seven-year-old from an anguished emptiness that had nearly made him physically sick.

We don't know where this new hold on the supernatural will take us. Crime figures are still frighteningly high, and widespread crime indicates grave sickness in the soul of a nation.

Alcohol and other drugs are still a too general alternative to facing life realistically, and the drug scene in America signals serious weakness in the character of a nation.

Where we go from here depends.

It depends on how long and vigorously the new generation of Christians continues to spread the Word and call for a radical turning to Christ, God's Son. (In His earthly life He was the world's number one supernaturalist.) It depends on whether their new faith makes them want to shoulder the world's troubles or hide from them. (The former appears to be the case.)

The opinion of one Christian statesman, now

dead, was that there are enough Christians ten times over to save a broken world from destruction and bring it to God — if they want to badly enough.